EXTREME CARS

Produced for HarperCollins by:

HYDRA PUBLISHING
129 MAIN STREET
IRVINGTON, NY 10533
WWW.HYLASPUBLISHING.COM

FIRST EDITION

The name of the "Smithsonian," "Smithsonian Institution," and the sunburst logo are registered trademarks of the Smithsonian Institution.

Library of Congress Cataloging-in-Publication Data

Travers, Jim.
  Extreme cars / Jim Travers. -- 1st ed.
      p. cm.
  Includes bibliographical references and index.
  ISBN 978-0-06-089144-2
  1. Motor vehicles--Technological innovations--History. 2. Automobiles--History. 3. Motor vehicles--Collectors and collecting. 4. Experimental automobiles--History. 5. Sports cars--History. I. Title.

  TL15.T73 2007
  629.222--dc22

      2007024638

07 08 09 10   QW   10 9 8 7 6 5 4 3 2 1

EXTREME
CARS

Collins
An Imprint of HarperCollinsPublishers

Jim Travers

Contents

From the Model T to the Moon

Just about 100 years have passed since the first Model T rolled out of the Ford factory in Detroit, Michigan, but various horseless carriages were built in small workshops and garages decades before Henry Ford's creation came along to put the world on wheels.

The oldest example in the Smithsonian Institution collection is a Dudgeon steam wagon dating from 1866. Designed and built by machinist Richard Dudgeon, the wagon was built as an effort by its designer to end the abuse and mistreatment of workhorses. Although never mass-produced, the Dudgeon was capable of speeds between 25 and 30 miles (40–48 km) per hour, could carry eight passengers, and was used by the machinist on the streets of Manhattan.

The purpose of this book, however, is not to be a chronology of the automobile. Rather, it is to take a look at some of the more extreme examples that have come along during the course of the past century or so—be they competition cars, rare cars, expensive cars, unique street cars, or experiments that never quite made it to the mainstream marketplace. Many are some combination of the above, like the Chrysler Turbine car of the 1960s. Fifty identical models were built, and one resides today in the Smithsonian collection.

The other reason for this book is to

Left: The Volkswagen Beetle was unique, practical, and reliable enough to remain in production for more than 50 years. It is an automotive icon, driven and recognized all over the world.

Below: Lambasted by Ralph Nader for serious safety defects, the Chevrolet Corvair had improved significantly by the time this 1965 model came out, but the car's reputation was tarnished and it was discontinued by 1969. Despite the many groundbreaking cars Detroit companies have contributed to the automotive world, they have also rolled out their share of panned or defective vehicles.

Above: Janet Guthrie was the first woman to compete in both the Indianapolis 500 and the Daytona 500.

Below: Porsche's most recent foray into the super-car field, the Carrera GT, can accelerate from 0–60 miles (0–97 km) per hour in 3.5 seconds.

cars are fascinating people.

This book also includes vehicles that have traveled to the farthest reaches of the globe, some operating in war zones and others used by Arctic explorers. You will find still others that have traveled over the sea, including both Mountbatten hovercrafts designed to skim across the English Channel carrying hundreds of passengers and the 1951 Chevrolet truck used by its pilot and his family and friends to flee Cuba across the treacherous Florida Straits.

In addition, you will find cars designed to float above the world, like the Moller Skycar—a combination car, airplane, and one man's life's work. There are cars that have traveled far beyond our world, including the Lunar Roving Vehicle commissioned by NASA to be the first wheeled transport for astronauts on the moon.

Some designs were good ideas that just arrived at the wrong time. America may have not been ready for the Cord 810 when it was first shown at the New York Auto Show in 1935, with front-wheel-drive and a low-slung design featuring hidden

look at the men and women behind the cars—and behind the wheel. Often, the characters associated with these cars are every bit as much of the story as the vehicles themselves. Whether they are inventors, race drivers, designers, or collectors, many of the individuals who choose to hang around

headlights. A design rushed to production by a company struggling to survive the Great Depression did not help, and quality control problems made matters worse. Timing, as the saying goes, is everything. This book is by no means a complete look at everything noteworthy ever to come down the pike in the automotive world. It is a series of random snapshots, including some cars you would expect to see in any book about cars, like the Volkswagen Beetle. It is also about some less known and maybe even less loved models. We have made room for the Little Red Wagon, the drag racing pickup truck that wowed audiences by traveling the length of a quarter mile strip with front wheels in the air, and even for the much-maligned Chevrolet Corvair.

We have undoubtedly left out some notable models worthy of mention, but again, this is but a collection of snapshots. Since the creators of the first car put down their wrenches and fired it up, untold thousands of models, and millions of cars have followed. It is easy to leave something out, so please forgive us if your personal favorite did not make the cut.

In the meantime, please settle in and take a ride in some extreme automobiles from today and yesterday. We hope you enjoy it.

The Gibbs Aquada can reach 100 miles (160.93 km) per hour on land and 30 miles (48.3 km/26.1 knots) per hour on water. Though a bit too pricey for the average consumer, the Aquada is an innovation in amphibious automobile technology. Here, Sir Richard Branson is at the controls for a voyage across the English Channel.

Chronology

1900
More than 100 American companies offer automobiles powered by gasoline, steam, or electricity. No one technology is dominant.

1901
New York becomes the first state to require that automobiles are registered.

1903
H. Nelson Jackson and Sewall Crocker become the first to cross the United States by car in a 1903 Winton.

1904
Only one-sixth of rural public roads have any kind of surfacing.

1906
Driver Fred Marriott pilots the steam-powered Stanley Rocket to a land speed record of 127.7 mph.

1908
The first Ford Model T is built. Within six years production increases to 250,000 cars annually.

1909
At the wheel of a Maxwell, Alice Huyler Ramsey is the first woman to drive across the United States.

1910
Gasoline-powered engines have become more popular than steam or electric engines, and take over as the engine of choice for buyers.

1913
The Lincoln Highway Association is formed to promote the building of a paved highway from New York to California.

1913
More than 4,000 people lose their lives in car accidents.

1918
All states now require license plates, but mandatory driver licensing and testing is still years away.

1919
100,000 Americans now make their living working in oil fields.

1920s
Cities install traffic towers where police officers can keep an eye on the road and operate traffic signals.

1920s
General Motors introduces the concept of car financing to the consumer.

1926
Route 66, running from Chicago to Los Angeles, is commissioned.

1930
23 million cars are now on the road, and more than half of American families own a car.

1930s
Many high schools now offer driver education. By this time, more than 30,000 annual deaths are attributed to car accidents.

1930s
The paving of The Lincoln Highway, the first transcontinental road across the United States, is completed. Thousands of family campgrounds spring up around the country as the travel-trailer craze begins.

1932
63,000 school buses are now on the road, signaling the end of the road for the one-room schoolhouse.

1932
Ford Motor Company introduces the first V8 engine in a car for the masses.

1934
Adolf Hitler outlines the specifications for his "People's car," later to become the Volkswagen Beetle. Production begins five years later, but is delayed by WWII.

1935
Thirty-nine states now require licenses for drivers, but few require a test.

1935
Parking meters are introduced in Oklahoma City.

1935
More than one third of rural roads are now surfaced, and many are paved with concrete and asphalt for motor traffic.

1935
More than 200,000 gas stations are operating nation-wide.

1936
First Oscar Mayer Wienermobile hits the road.

1945
Suburbia blossoms following World War II, as mobile Americans leave cities in search of a better life.

1946
Volkswagen Beetle production resumes.

1948
Park Forest, Illinois opens, a planned community more than 30 miles from downtown Chicago. Within two years, it has more than 8,000 residents.

1953
Chevrolet Corvette is introduced.

1956
Congress passes the Federal-Aid Highway Act, giving birth to the 41,000-mile interstate system. The plan was to link America's cities by roads designed for travel at speeds up to 70 miles per hour.

1958
Ford Motor Company introduces the Edsel. Sales are far worse than projected, and never improve.

1959
Volvo introduces the first three-point shoulder harness, now standard on all cars and credited with saving more lives than any other auto-safety device.

1960
The Chevrolet Corvair is launched. It wins the Motor Trend Car of the Year award. Safety issues will later lead to its demise.

1963
Chrysler builds 50 experimental turbine powered cars for the street, and puts them into daily use by ordinary families.

1964
The Ford Mustang is introduced at the New York World's Fair. 22,000 are sold the first day. Hertz begins renting high performance Shelby GT350-H models the following year.

1966
Congress passes the National Highway Safety Act, the first U.S. Government effort to mandate safer automobiles.

1970
Volkswagen sells more than 560,000 cars in the United States, most of them Beetles. VW market share in the U.S. is seven percent.

1970
The Ford Pinto and Chevrolet Vega, four-cylinder small cars intended to combat imports, are introduced as 1971 models. Both are plagued with quality problems.

1973
An embargo on oil shipments to the U.S. by the Organization of Petroleum Exporting Countries (OPEC) creates a gasoline shortage. Motorists are faced with gas rationing, and Congress lowers the national speed limit to 55 miles (89 km) per hour.

1978
General Motors produces its first passenger car powered by a diesel engine. A class-action lawsuit on behalf of angry buyers follows.

1980
Annual sales of Japanese cars reach two million units in the United States, amounting to 20 percent of all new car sales.

1983
Chrysler introduces the first minivans.

1996
General Motors begins leasing the electric-powered EV1 to customers.

1999
Honda builds the first FCX, a hydrogen powered passenger car.

2000
The gasoline/electric hybrid Toyota Prius is launched.

2007
Three women drivers start the Indianapolis 500 for the first time in history: Danica Patrick, Sarah Fisher, and Milka Duno.

Records

Land Speed Records					
Rank	Car	Driver	Country	Date	Speed
1	Thrust SSC	Andy Green	Great Britain	October 15, 1997	766.609 mph (1233.74 km/h)
2	Thrust 2	Richard Noble	Great Britain	October 4, 1983	633.470 mph (1019.47 km/h)
3	Blue Flame	Gary Gabelich	USA	October 23, 1970	622.407 mph (1001.67 km/h)
4	Spirit of America	Craig Breedlove	USA	November 15, 1965	600.601 mph (966.57 km/h)
5	Goldenrod	Bob Summers	USA	November 13, 1965	409.277 mph (658.67 km/h)

Early Land Speed Records

In 1903, Barney Oldfield became the first driver to circuit a one-mile (1.6 km) track at 60 miles (97 km) per hour. In 1906, driving the steam-powered Stanley Rocket, Fred Marriott became the first person to travel two miles (3.2 km) per minute in any vehicle. Two hours later, he set a new land speed record in the same car, at 127.6 miles (205.4 km) per hour.

Coast to Coast Driving

H. Nelson Jackson and Sewall Crocker, driving a 1903 Winton, became the first people to cross the United States by car. The trip took them a little over two months. In 1915, Erwin "Cannonball" Baker set a new record for cross-country automotive travel by making it from San Diego to New York City in 11 days, 7 hours, and 15 minutes at the wheel of a Stutz Bearcat. In 1933, Baker obliterated his record by crossing the country in 53 hours and 30 minutes in a Graham-Paige Model 57 Blue Streak 8. In 1979, Dave Heinz and Dave Yarborough set the current documented American coast-to-coast driving record of 32 hours and 51 minutes in a Jaguar XJS.

Longest Production

Volkswagen Beetle production began in 1939, only to be promptly interrupted by World War II. Production resumed in 1946, and some 22 million models were built until production ceased in 2003, making the Beetle the longest running model in automotive history.

Most Expensive Cars Sold at Auction			
Rank	Name	Date	Price
1	1931 Bugatti Royale Kellner Coupe	November 1987	$8,700,000
2	1929 Mercedes-Benz 38/250 SSK	September 2004	$7,443,070
3	1931 Bugatti Royale Berline De Voyager	June 1986	$6,500,000
4	1962 Ferrari 330 TRI/LM Testa Rossa	August 2002	$6,490,000
5	1966 Ferrari 330 P3	August 2000	$5,616,000
6	1962 Ferrari 250 GTO	November 1991	$5,500,000
7	1930 Bentley Speed Six	July 2004	$5,109,700
8	1935 Duesenberg SJ Speedster	August 2004	$5,109,700
9	1937 Alfa-Romeo 8C-2900	August 1999	$4,072,000
10	1956 Ferrari 410 Sport	August 2001	$3,822,500

Largest Vehicle Collections

Waste-management tycoon Harold LeMay built the largest car collection in the United States, including some 3,000 cars, trucks, and other vehicles. The Sultan of Brunei, Hassanal Bolkiah, is said to own roughly 3,000 to 5,000 automobiles, many of them one-of-a-kind supercars.

A Record for Safety

The three-point safety belt, introduced by Volvo in 1959 and eventually utilized by all major automakers, is credited with saving more lives than any other automotive safety device.

Highest Mileage for a Passenger Car

With over two million miles (three million km) driven, Irv Gordon's 1965 Volvo P1800 coupe has the highest mileage for a passenger car. As of this writing, the Volvo is still on the road.

Super Supercar

In 2003, Bugatti Veyron production began. The Veyron broke a handful of records at once. With a top speed of more than 250 miles (402.3 km) per hour, it is the fastest passenger car in the world. Its 1,001 horsepower make it the most powerful production car, and with a price tag of one million dollars, it is also the most expensive.

Women Racers at the Indy 500

In 1977, Janet Guthrie became the first woman to compete in the Indianapolis 500. In 2005, Danica Patrick finished fourth at the Indianapolis 500, the best finish by a woman in the history of the race. In 2007, three women drivers competed in the Indianapolis 500 for the first time in history. Danica Patrick finished in eighth place.

Above: Bobby Rahal congratulates Danica Patrick after her fourth-place finish in the 2005 Indy 500.

Opposite page: The Thrust SSC, driven by Andy Green, hurtles toward its record land speed of 766.609 mph (1233.74 km/h).

Fastest Production Cars		
Car	Date	Speed
Bugatti Veyron	October, 2005	253.2 mph (407.5 km/h)
Koenigsegg CCR	February 28, 2005	241.01 mph (387.87 km/h)
McLaren F1	March 31, 1998	240.1 mph (386.4 km/h) with factory rev limiter removed
McLaren F1	1994	231 mph (372 km/h) at factory rev limit
RUF CTR (modified Porsche 930)	1987	211 mph (340 km/h)

CARS THAT GO TO EXTREMES

PART 1

CHAPTER 1

SUPERCARS

FOR AS LONG AS there have been automobiles, there has been intense competition among carmakers to build the fastest car on the street. It is all well and good to hold records at Bonneville or on a racetrack, but street cars are the models most recognized—and likely purchased—by people in the market for a sports car. That recognition cannot only help sell a certain model, it can spice up interest in an automaker's entire product lineup.

Some folks buy supercars as showpieces or for their cachet as status symbols. Others truly enjoy driving them. Periods of supercar building wax and wane, but over the past few years, the horsepower wars have grown more intense, with manufacturers offering street cars faster than many race cars of recent memory. High-tech body materials like carbon fiber have increased strength while reducing weight, and computerized engine controls—combined with systems like electronic stability control, traction control, and antilock brakes—have made it possible to deliver tremendous performance with little fuss. Engines with 500 horsepower are not uncommon among today's supercars, and both styling and engineering have become incredibly refined.

Here is a look at some of the fastest supercars available today.

Left: The fastest production car in the world, the Bugatti Veyron has a top speed of over 250 miles (402.34 km) per hour. Inset: The Enzo Ferrari, the legendary company's latest supercar. All models were sold before the first car was even built. Pages 8–9: In the early 1960's, Chrysler built 55 experimental turbine cars to test the viability of such technology. Though groundbreaking, turbine engines were ultimately deemed impractical.

McLaren F1

The designers of the McLaren F1 had a simple, but ambitious goal in 1993: to create the finest high-performance road car ever built, or likely ever to be built. Drawing on McLaren Automotive's decades of Formula One, IndyCar, and Can-Am race car building experience, the F1 was the first production car to use an all-carbon composite monocoque, a fused body and chassis that is lightweight and incredibly strong.

To ensure both outstanding performance and daily drivability, McLaren turned to BMW, who designed and built the S70/2 engine specifically for the F1. The 6.1-liter, quad-cam, 48-valve V12 produced 627 horsepower and was matched with a six-speed transaxle gearbox. The result was a 2,513-pound land-

With all doors, hoods, and hatches open, the F1 looks less like a supercar than a spaceship.

SPECIFICATIONS

MCLAREN F1
Top speed: 240.1 mph (386 km/h)
0–60 mph (0–97 km/h): 3.2 sec
1/4 mile (0.4 km): 11.1 sec at 138 mph (222 km/h)
Engine: Custom-built 6.1 liter, quad-cam,
   48-valve, 12-cyl BMW S70/2 engine
   rated at 618 hp (461 kw) at 7500 rpm,
   and 480 lb ft (650 nm) of torque at
   5,600 rpm

rocket capable of zero to 60 miles (0-97 km) per hour in 3.2 seconds, and a quarter-mile (0.4 km) time of 11.1 seconds. The price? A nice, round, one million dollars.

The F1 driver sits in the center of the cockpit, flanked by two passenger seats offset slightly to the rear. Each car was tailor made for its owner, and McLaren planted each driver's seat in the best position for him or her to reach the controls. In addition to creature comforts like a CD stereo and air-conditioning, every F1 came with a set of custom handmade leather luggage, made to fit in the car's luggage compartments. Keeping true to its race car heritage, the stereo was a special lightweight unit, and the complimentary tool kit was made of lightweight titanium.

The F1 really is a race car let loose on the street. Only 100 were built during a production run that began

"I don't think so, there's no one at McLaren who can weld that badly."

—GORDON MURRAY, DESIGNER OF THE McLAREN F1,
ON IF IT WOULD RESEMBLE THE FERRARI F40.

them especially collectible and nearly impossible to find. However, the factory will be happy to let any interested parties know if an F1 becomes available, and will remount the seat, repaint the car, and even reoption or rebuild it as well as deliver a new set of luggage. McLaren's customer care does not end there, though. If your F1 is experiencing problems that your local Authorized Service Center cannot remedy, each F1 has been equipped with a modem to enable McLaren technicians to diagnose problem cars found nearly anywhere around the world. If issues still arise, the company will fly out a technician. No worries once you put your name on that waiting list. Just keep the checkbook handy.

Left: A rare sight: a McLaren F1 parked on a city street. If you missed your chance to buy one of the 64 F1 road cars, McLaren will help you find one. However, expect to pay more than the original $1,000,000 price tag.

Below: The F1 driver sits in the center of the car, with seats for two passengers to the left and the right.

in 1993 and ended in 1998. Only 64 of those were strictly road cars. Of the other 36, most were built for customers competing in the 24 Hours of Le Mans or F1 GTR races. In March 1998, an F1 earned the title of fastest production car in the world, reaching 240 miles (398 km) per hour. The F1 held this record until 2005—an especially impressive run given the dramatic recent increases in automakers' performance wars.

The fact that no more than 64 of these road cars will ever exist makes

Lamborghini Murciélago LP640

With a top speed of more than 211 miles per hour and capable of a zero to 60 miles (0–97 km) per hour sprint in less than three and a half seconds, the Lamborghini Murciélago is no slouch. And at about $320,000, it does not come cheap, although its price tag actually makes it something of a mid-priced supercar.

In exchange for its ostentatious performance, the Murciélago returns 11 miles per gallon (4.67 km/l) in combined highway and city driving according to the Environmental Protection Agency. Owners limited to a city-only motoring experience can expect about nine miles per gallon. Either way, expect to be buying premium gasoline. Anybody who can pony up the sticker price probably

does not care, but the Murciélago is not designed to run on regular.

Named for a legendary Spanish fighting bull, the Murciélago's power comes from a 6.5-liter, V12 engine producing 633 horsepower and driving all four wheels. The engine is mounted lengthwise just behind the two seats, which explains the LP in its name: *longitudinale posteriori*. For buyers concerned that the extroverted styling the LP640 wears in stock trim will not draw quite enough attention, an optional transparent engine cover should seal the deal.

The transmission is a six-speed manual; an electronically shifted automatic "e-gear" gearbox, with steering wheel mounted paddle shifters, is optional.

Between Lamborghini's trademark

The Murciélago LP640 is hardly a car for wallflowers, with in-your-face styling to match its 633 horsepower.

SPECIFICATIONS

LAMBORGHINI MURCIÉLAGO LP640

Top speed: 210 mph (339 km/h)
0–62 mph (0–100 km/h): 3.4 sec
1/4 mile (0.4 km): 11.1 sec at 124 mph
(235 km/h)
Engine: 6.5 liter V12 rated at 633 hp (472 kw)
at 8,000 rpm and 487 lb ft (660 nm)
of torque at 6,000 rpm

Left: The LP640's engine is longitudinally mounted, meaning that the engine's crankshaft is oriented front to back, rather than side to side. In addition, the LP640's transmission is located at the very back of the car, instead of towards the middle, as is common among supercars.

Below: The protruding rear intake vents of the LP460 open automatically as the engine's temperature rises.

scissors doors lies a luxurious interior, with leather upholstery, a DVD player, and MP3 capability. If the standard interior is not up to snuff, buyers can opt for a personalized look from the factory with Lamborghini's Privilegio customization program.

An aluminum space frame and combination steel and carbon-fiber bodywork help keep the Murciélago's weight down to a still not-insubstantial 3,671 pounds (1,665 kg). Not that the Lambo's weight does much to slow

its blistering performance—just ask any automotive journalist who has survived a test drive. Not generally known for their driving skills, car writers have reportedly been responsible for totaling at least two LP640s, which only went on sale in spring 2006. Considering that the original Murciélago, with a meager 500 horsepower, went on sale in 2001 and that around 2,000 total have been sold in its five years of existence, the journalists have quite literally made a dent in the new LP640's production.

Saleen S7

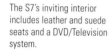

The S7's inviting interior includes leather and suede seats and a DVD/Television system.

Steve Saleen and his crew took a distinctly American approach to supercar building with the S7: they just modernized an old idea. The notion of combining a thumping pushrod V8 with lightened bodywork has been around since the earliest days of hot-rodding, and like a lot of good ideas, it has not gotten old—especially when the pushrod V8 uses the latest technology and is a 7.0-liter, all-aluminum monster with twin turbochargers pumping out 750 horsepower. It also cannot hurt performance that Saleen makes liberal use of aluminum in everything from the structure to the suspension and brakes, along with carbon-fiber body panels, to help keep weight down to just 2,950 pounds (1,338 kg).

The resulting performance from this mid-engine two-seater is what one might expect, and then some: Zero to 60 miles (96.5 km) per hour is achieved in a claimed 2.8 seconds, and a quarter-mile (0.4 km) is over in just 10.5

SPECIFICATIONS

SALEEN S7 TWIN TURBO
Top speed: 248 mph (399 km/h) [manufacturer's claim]
0–60 mph (0–97 km/h): 2.8 sec
1/4 mile (0.4 km): 10.5 sec at 145 mph (233 km/h)
Engine: Twin-turbocharged V8 with aluminum block and heads rated at 750 hp (559 kw) at 6,300 rpm, and 700 lb ft (948 nm) of torque at 4,800 rpm

seconds—at 145 miles (233 km) per hour. Top speed is listed at "over 200" miles (more than 322 km) per hour. The price is $580,000 unless you opt for the optional polished wheels and navigation system.

Standard equipment includes a leather steering wheel, as well as leather and suede seats. The driver's seating position is custom fitted. Specially sized luggage is also included—probably a good idea, because despite having trunks front and rear, the S7 has only 5.47 cubic feet (0.1549 cu. m) of trunk space. A rearview video camera with an LCD display helps the driver keep an eye on the cars and objects left in the S7's wake. A 240-miles (386 km) per hour speedometer is part of the package, and entertainment equipment includes a DVD/Television system, along with the expected AM/FM radio and CD player. More mundane but appreciated equipment includes

air-conditioning, a tilting-and-telescoping steering wheel, keyless remote, a heated windshield, and power windows, locks, and mirrors.

Like some other supercars, the S7 was developed with racing in mind. Wind tunnel-derived aerodynamic touches include as many body vents as possible, to help air flow through the car. Even the underside was developed to help air flow past as smoothly as possible. Following the introduction of the S7R, the competition version, in October 2000, it went on to win the prestigious Twelve Hours of Sebring in early 2001. By the end of that year, S7Rs had racked up four more championships in both the United States and Europe. Its extensive racing history includes more than 60 pole positions, and Saleen race cars have captured wins at such legendary tracks as Daytona, Florida; Silverstone in Great Britain; Barcelona, Spain; and Monza, Italy.

If all this sounds good, act fast to drive fast. Saleen builds only 25 examples of the S7 per year.

Above: The S7's huge 7.0-liter V8 engine is visible beneath the rear window.

Below: As fast as it looks standing still, the S7 is even faster with the accelerator down. Zero to 60 miles (96.5 km) per hour comes up in less than three seconds.

Enzo Ferrari

Ferrari may well be the most recognized exotic car builder in the world, so when the Italian carmaker decides to make a limited-edition supercar, it is bound to be something special.

The Enzo of 2002 was such a car. Following in the tire tracks of exceptional Ferraris like the limited production F40 and F50, the Enzo was named for Signor Ferrari himself, the company's founder, and enthusiasts are quick to point out that the car is an Enzo Ferrari, not a Ferrari Enzo.

A classic before it ever spun a tire, the Enzo was announced at the Paris Auto Show in 2002, and original plans called for a run of 349

cars. Invitations to purchase one were sent out to Ferrari owners, and all were spoken for before the first one was built—and before the $643,330 price was even announced. In response to demand, an additional 50 cars were added to production. In 2005, a final Enzo was built and auctioned to benefit victims of the devastating Asian Tsunami of 2004. Production ended after that 400th car, which sold for more than twice its list price.

Powered by a lightweight, racing-inspired 650 horsepower, 6.0-liter V12 with 48 valves and four overhead cams, Enzos were built with a six-speed, sequentially paddle-shifted manual transmission. A development goal was to shave shift times to just 150 milliseconds. Rated at twelve miles per gallon (5.10 km/l) highway and just eight miles per gallon (3.40 km/l) city, fuel mileage apparently had little impact on sales. Buyers who snapped

Above: The Enzo's Formula One-inspired V12 engine is rated at 650 horsepower.

Below: The legendary Italian automobile design firm Pininfarina designed the Enzo. Ferrari offered the supercar only to pre-existing Ferrari owners. All 349 planned for production were spoken for before the first one was built, despite the $643,330 price.

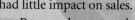

SPECIFICATIONS

ENZO FERRARI

Top speed: 218 mph (351 km/h)
0–60 mph (0–97 km/h): 3.3 sec
1/4 mile (0.4 km): 11.1 sec at 133 mph
   (222 km/h)
Engine: F140 65° V12 with four valves per
   cylinder, dual overhead cams, and
   variable valve timing rated at 650 hp
   (485 kw) at 7,800 rpm and 485 lb ft
   (657 nm) of torque at 5,500 rpm

up the limited run were probably more interested in performance than economy, and the Enzo delivered the goods. Quickly. The Enzo jumps from zero to 60 miles (0–97 km) per hour in only 3.3 seconds, and an Enzo has been clocked at 218 miles (351 km) per hour. A standing-start quarter-mile (0.4 km) takes just 11.1 seconds.

Ferrari dipped into extensive Formula One racing knowledge to build the Enzo, using carbon fiber not only for the body but also for the brake discs. Its styling blends form and function, and was heavily influenced by wind tunnel- and track testing. Active aerodynamics help keep the car planted at speed by increasing the angle of the rear wing when the Enzo zooms above 186 miles (299 km) per hour.

The list of Enzo owners reads like a who's who of movie and rock stars, captains of industry, sheiks, and the usual smattering of ambiguous characters. Most notable of the last group may be an individual in California who notoriously broke an Enzo in half while traveling the Pacific Coast Highway in Malibu, California, at what might be described as an antisocial rate of speed. Not only did he live to tell about it, he claimed that a mysterious acquaintance named Dietrich had been behind the wheel at the time. Dietrich was nowhere to be found after the crash.

Below: Seven-time Formula One World Champion Michael Schumacher takes the Enzo for a spin. Schumacher aided Ferrari in the development of the Enzo.

Background: Admirers catching a glimpse of the Enzo's distinctive bodywork.

Porsche Carrera GT

Porsche designers have always subscribed to the notion that carrying less weight is a key to performance, and the ultimate road-going Porsche of 2004–05 took that concept to a higher level. Constructed of a lightweight carbon-fiber monocoque with body panels of the same material, even the GT's seats are a combination of carbon-fiber and aramid fibers. The entire chassis weighs in at only 220 pounds (99.8 kg).

Power, of course, is also a key to performance, and the GT is covered in that department as well. With a 5.7-liter, 10-cylinder engine pumping out 612 horsepower to propel the Carrera's 3,037 pounds (1,377.6 kg), performance is scorching: zero to 62 mph (100 km) comes up in just 3.9 seconds,

SPECIFICATIONS

PORSCHE CARRERA GT
Top speed: 205 mph (330 km/h)
0--100 km/h (0–62 mph): 3.9 sec
1/4 mile (0.4 km): 11.2 sec at 133 mph (214 km/h)
Engine: 5.7 liter, aluminum V10 rated at 612 hp
  (456 kw) at 8,000 rpm and 435 lb ft (589 nm) of
  torque at 5,750 rpm

and top speed is 205 miles (329.9 km) per hour, making the Carrera GT the most powerful street Porsche ever built.

The transmission is a six-speed manual, matched with the first ceramic composite clutch ever used in an automobile—again, to save weight and space. Porsches are known for comfortable interiors, and the ultimate Porsche is no exception. The ultra-light 23.6-pound (10.71 kg) seats are covered with supple leather, and hand-crafted aluminum, wood, and magnesium surfaces round out the interior. Even the

Above: The Carrera GT's luxurious cabin includes a wooden shift knob reminiscent of the balsa shift knob in the 1970 Le Mans-winning Porsche 917.

Right: With 612 horsepower, the Carrera GT is the most powerful road-going Porsche ever built. However, a planned production run of 1,500 units was cut short due to slow sales.

of America boasts about 100,000 primary and affiliate members, and there are plenty of drivers around the world who share their enthusiam. Still, a planned production run of 1,500 units ended after only 1,270 units were built. Maybe by then everybody who wanted a $460,400 GT already had one. Maybe Porsche decided to devote resources elsewhere. Still, the number produced makes the GT one of the more successful supercars ever built. And as of this writing, one dealer in the Midwest still had a brand-new 2005 model available. The price? $424,995.

Left: The Carrera GT was built with an emphasis on lightness. Carbon fiber was widely used, from the body panels to the seats, to the chassis, which weighs only 220 pounds (99.8 kg).

Below: Supposedly, building each 959 cost Porsche twice as much as the $225,000 sale price. However, the carmaker probably should have kept a few models for themselves. The cars are worth more than $1,000,000 today.

door handles are molded magnesium.

For all of its exotica, building the Carrera GT was something of a stretch for a comparatively small, independent manufacturer like Porsche. The company needed to count on a certain number of sales before embarking on this technological tour de force. To that end, sales and development teams worked in tandem to make the Carrera GT a reality. As one official put it at the time, enough customers had to be prepared to "dig deep into their pockets" to justify building the supercar.

Fortunately, Porsche enthusiasts are a dedicated bunch. The Porsche Club

PORSCHE 959

Considered by some to be Porsche's first true supercar, the 959 of 1986–89 offered more than blistering performance. At the time, it was generally regarded as the most technologically advanced sports car ever built.

The 959 featured the first use of all-wheel drive in a high-performance car, and the effectiveness of the system so impressed Porsche executives that it became the basis of the Carrera 4 and is believed to have extended the life of the aging 911 series.

Powered by a 2.6-liter, air-cooled flat six equipped with twin turbochargers, the 959 produces 450 horsepower, enough to propel the 2,900-pound (1,313 kg) car from zero to 60 miles (96 km) per hour in 3.6 seconds. The $225,000 price tag is said to be less than half what it cost Porsche to build each of the roughly 270 produced.

Never street legal in the United States, a few 959s were imported by wealthy collectors anyway. A 1999 change in U.S. import laws has enabled individuals to modify their 959s for street use, but most still sit in storage. With values over a million dollars, why risk it?

Koenigsegg CCX

Sweden's automobile industry is usually associated with sensible, safe, practical cars like Volvos and Saabs, long on air bags and crash-worthiness, but not exactly the sexiest or fastest vehicles on the road.

Enter Koenigsegg, a lesser-known Swedish automaker that is quietly cranking out 25 examples per year of what is currently the second fastest car in production anywhere—the awe-inspiring, slightly less than Volvo-practical Koenigsegg CCX.

The independent manufacturer has been building variants of the CC (which stands for Competition Coupe) design since 1996. The new CCX is notable not only for its incredible performance; it is the first Koenigsegg design engineered to comply with American safety and emissions standards. Changes for

The body and chassis of the CCX are made of lightweight carbon fiber composite. Shoppers concerned with maximum weight savings will be relieved to hear that the 2,600-pound (1,179 kg) CCX can also be purchased with optional carbon fiber wheels that shave 6 pounds each from the weight of the car.

SPECIFICATIONS

KOENIGSEGG CCX
Top speed: 250 mph (403 km/h)
0–100 km/h (0–62 mph): 3.2 sec
1/4 mile (0.4 km): 9.9 sec at 146 mph (235 km/h)
Engine: Cast aluminum, 4,700 cu cm DOHC 32-valve V8 with twin Rotrex centrifugal superchargers rated at 806 hp (601 kw) at 6,900 rpm and 678 lb ft (918 nm) of torque at 5,700 rpm on 91 octane (US rating) gasoline

U.S. sale include lengthening the car by three inches (7.62 cm) to comply with impact regulations. Koenigsegg also has redesigned lighting, and engineered a cleaner burning engine designed to have the same blistering performance of previous CC models not available stateside.

Top speed for the CCX is listed on the Koenigsegg web site at more than 245 miles (394 km) per hour, and zero to 60 mph (96 km/h) is reached in just 3.2 seconds. A quarter mile (0.4 km) comes up in 9.9 seconds, by which time the CCX will be traveling at 146 miles (235.97 km) per hour.

In a unique nod to the needs of taller drivers, Koenigsegg boasts that the CCX has two inches (5.08 cm)

more headroom than previous CC variants, which they say makes it the most spacious supercar on the market—something for which ultra high-performance cars are not usually known.

The CCX gets its power from an 806-horsepower, aluminum block V8 with four valves per cylinder, double overhead camshafts, and twin superchargers. Extensively redesigned for the U.S. market, with new cylinder heads and other components, Koenigsegg says that the CCX's engine is their first engine to be engineered and assembled entirely in-house.

To keep weight down, both the body and chassis are made of lightweight carbon fiber composite, reinforced with Kevlar and aluminum honeycomb. Optional carbon fiber wheels can be ordered for owners concerned

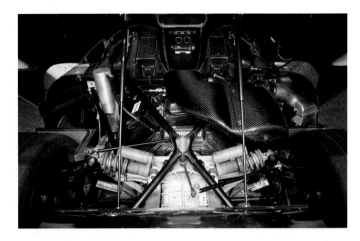

about shaving an additional six and a half pounds from the standard magnesium wheels. Seat frames are also of carbon fiber, and the entire CCX weighs just 2,601 pounds (1,179.8 kg).

In the interest of coddling fast-moving folks of all statures, the CCX comes with leather seating and can be had with custom luggage. For the practical, the CCX will run on 91-octane (U.S. rated) fuel.

And even with all its performance, the CCX does remain true to its Swedish heritage. The carmaker claims it has done well in the safety crash tests required for domestic sales.

Above: The CCX's potent aluminum block V8 gets 806 horsepower, and in a feat of engineering can run on either U.S. rated 91 or 95 octane gasoline (European rated 110 octane), or biofuel.

Left: The CCX is the third production supercar made by Koenigsegg, a company founded in Sweden in 1994 with the goal of making world-class, record breaking supercars.

Bugatti Veyron 16.4

In the over-the-top world of super-cars, they just do not come any further over the top than this: 1,001 horsepower, a top speed of more than 250 miles (402.34 km) per hour, and zero to 60 (96 km) in two and a half seconds—all for just one million dollars and change.

The name Bugatti has long been associated with elegant, technically sophisticated sports and racing cars. Bugattis from the 1920s and 1930s remain some of the most highly sought-after collector cars today, regarded for their technical sophistication and prized as works of art.

In 1998, when Volkswagen purchased the rights to the name of Ettore Bugatti's long-defunct automobile company, part of the company's plan to reintroduce the Bugatti name was by building the ultimate supercar.

Below: In 2000, Volkswagen chairman Ferdinand Piëch announced that the company was going to build the fastest and most expensive supercar ever made. After six years of tumultuous development, the Veyron emerged, meeting all of Piëch's claims, and exceeding the expectations of many naysayers.

Background: At full throttle, it is said that the Veyron will empty a full tank of gasoline in 12 minutes. However, the supercar could probably coast quite a distance from 250 mph (402 km/h).

SPECIFICATIONS

BUGATTI VEYRON 16.4
Top speed: 253 mph (407 km/h)
0–60 mph (0–97 km/h): 2.5 sec
1/4 mile (0.4 km): 10.2 sec at 143 mph (230 km/h)
Engine: Aluminum, quad-turbocharged, intercooled DOHC 64-valve W-16 rated at 1,001 hp (746 kw) at 6,000 rpm, and 922 lb ft (1,249 nm) of torque at 2,200 rpm

Hand-built at a rate of just 70 cars a year, the carbon-fiber monocoque Veyron is a worthy tribute to Mr. Bugatti. It is technically sophisticated right down to the last detail—even the fastening screws are made of titanium.

The heart of the 16.4 is its eight-liter, 64-valve engine with four turbochargers. Unique among modern cars for its number of cylinders, the engine is notable for its layout as well. It is called a W16, meaning there are four rows of four pistons each, arranged in two banks of eight cylinders. Think of two V8 engines joined side by side and using a single crankshaft. The resulting 1,001 horsepower gives the Veyron the distinction

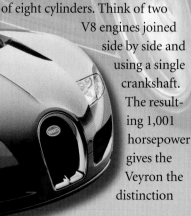

of having the most powerful engine ever installed in a production automobile. That is, if you call it a production automobile. With just 300 units planned from the start, Bugatti prefers to call it a vehicle built in series.

To translate all that power to the street, the Veyron uses all-wheel drive and a sequentially shifted, seven-speed, double-clutch DSG transmission that works either manually or automatically and shifts in two-tenths of a second.

One of the design challenges to building the Veyron was developing fuel pumps capable of feeding the W16. The engine's appetite for gasoline is so voracious at full throttle that a driver with his or her foot planted firmly to the plush carpet would run out of fuel in only 12 minutes. The good news is, at 250 miles (402.34 km) per hour, one would travel about 50 miles during those 12 minutes—most likely a sufficient distance to find a gas station.

The Veyron has three different suspension settings—standard, handling, and top speed. The settings change variables like ride height, spoiler deployment and airflow, depending on the speed of the vehicle. To access the Top Speed setting, necessary if your plans include travel faster than 233 miles (374.98 km) per hour, a second key, located next to the driver's seat, must be turned. For those who just have to

know, the Veyron has a gauge to indicate just how much of its 1,001 horsepower is being used at any given time.

Going fast is fun, but stopping on your own terms has its rewards. To that end, the Veyron has 15.7-inch (39.9 cm) carbon/ceramic brake discs with four pads in front, and 15-inch (38.1 cm) discs in the rear. To help slow the car from high speed, the Veyron's rear spoiler doubles as an air brake.

The Veyron was designed to be both the ultimate in performance and luxury. The interior is finished in hand-stitched leather, and features finely machined and polished aluminum pieces reminiscent of classic Bugattis. While equipped with creature comforts like a high-end sound system and climate control, you will not find a complicated on-board computer or multifunction control system. Keeping the emphasis on performance, the Veyron forgoes excessive cockpit gadgetry, allowing the driver to focus on piloting the car.

Above: The Veyron's massive 16-cylinder, 64-valve engine.

Below: The Veyron's interior incorporates designs reminiscent of classic Bugattis.

Chevrolet Corvette Z06

The 505-horsepower Z06 is something of a sleeper among supercars. Compared to some others in this group, its looks are downright conservative. Casual observers might not even be able to tell it apart from any other Corvette. But a closer look reveals that the fastest, most powerful, and technologically advanced Corvette ever built has few body panels in common with lesser models, giving just a hint of the performance that lies within.

At a base price of about $70,000, the Z06 is also something of a bargain in high-performance motoring. Assuming, of course, you can find one available at sticker price. Some less- than-scrupulous dealers have reportedly been tacking on substantial surcharges, and speculators started ordering and advertising cars at inflated prices

before the first one even arrived in a showroom.

Still, this ultimate Vette's performance figures rival those of cars costing two, three, and even ten times as much: It accelerates zero to 60 miles (0–97 km) per hour in 3.6 seconds, a quarter mile (0.4 km) passes by in 11.7 seconds, and it can reach a top speed of 198 miles (318.65 km) per hour. Maximum lateral acceleration exceeds 1 g, and the Z06 stops from 60 miles (97 km) per hour in just 111.3 feet. All this, and the Z06 earned an EPA rating of 26 miles per gallon (11 km/l) on the highway. Attention bargain hunters: Not only is the Z06's mileage better than other cars with this kind of performance, it is good enough to make the ultimate Vette exempt from the gas-guzzler tax—highly unusual for a supercar.

With 505 horsepower on tap and a sticker price hundreds of thousands of dollars less than its supercar peers, the Z06 is serious speed at a bargain.

SPECIFICATIONS

CHEVROLET CORVETTE Z06
Top speed: 198 mph (318.65 km/h)
0–60 mph (0–97 km/h): 3.6 sec
1/4 mile (0.4 km): 11.7 sec at 125 mph
(225 km/h)
Engine: 7-liter LS7 aluminum-block V8 rated
at 505 hp (377 kw) at 6,300 rpm, and
470 lb ft (637 nm) of torque at 4,800 rpm

Powered by a 427-cubic-inch, 7.0-liter V8 unique to the Z06, the LS7 engine gets a different block casting with a larger bore than other Corvettes. Other high-performance tidbits include titanium connecting rods and intake valves, cast-aluminum pistons, a forged steel crankshaft and main bearing caps, and racing-derived aluminum cylinder heads. An upgraded six-speed manual transmission delivers power to the rear wheels. Brakes are four-wheel discs, with 14-inch (35.56 cm) front rotors and 13.4-inch (34.03 cm) rears. Six separate brake pads supply stopping power to each front wheel.

Special body panels were developed from the Le Mans-winning Corvette race car. A new hood features a cold air intake, and the front fenders are carbon fiber, with air extractors behind each front wheel. Rear fenders are widened, with flares to cover the widest tires ever installed on a Corvette.

For all of its blistering performance, the Z06 is a remarkably civilized car to drive around town. A leather interior and creature comforts like dual-zone air-conditioning, a six-CD changer, and a navigation system help keep things civilized, and engine management controls make the Z06 docile in normal driving. But jab the throttle, and the ultimate Corvette's race-car heritage comes roaring out.

Above: The 427-cubic-inch, LS7 V8 engine.

Below: The unmistakable two by two taillights of a Corvette are easy to identify as the car accelerates past you on the highway.

CHAPTER 2

EXTREME RACE CARS

A GENERALLY ACCEPTED NOTION among just about anybody associated with racing, whether fans in the cheap seats or owners of multimillion-dollar race teams, is that auto racing has been around pretty much since the construction of a second car made it possible to race against somebody.

Brothers Francis Edgar and Freelan Oscar Stanley were some of automobile racing's earliest pioneers. After building a steam-powered competition cycle in 1898, they went on to build their first racing car in 1903. Stanley Steamers went on to become the fastest vehicles of their time, going on to set land speed records.

Of the thousands of wheeled racing vehicles since produced, some stand out more than others. Most competition cars are designed to comply with the rigid rules of one category or another and end up fading into obscurity after their days in the sun. Some survive for a few seasons, but advancing technology will always put them on the trailer for good after a while.

Others become legends, better known than their designers, drivers, and sponsors would have imagined in their wildest dreams. Not all have checkered histories, but some become favorites with fans, some have broken tradition, and some have changed the rules.

Louis Ross barreling down Daytona Beach in a Stanley Steamer in 1903.

Stanley Steamer

In the early 1900s, steam-powered automobiles were a popular alternative to cars with gasoline engines. Their relative simplicity and fewer moving parts made them quieter, smoother, faster, and more reliable than their gas-powered competition. At the turn of the twentieth century, buyers could choose from more than 125 different makers of steam vehicles. The Stanley Steamer is probably the most widely remembered of these.

Twin brothers Francis Edgar Stanley and Freelan Oscar Stanley were already successful industrialists and inventors when they founded the Stanley Motor Carriage Company in the city of Newton, Massachusetts. Francis had invented the airbrush and a photographic plate-coating process that the brothers later sold to George Eastman of Kodak fame. The brothers were also racing enthusiasts who built their first steam-powered competition cycle in 1898. Their first automobile was intended for personal use, but it created such a stir that the recently retired brothers found themselves in the car business with orders for 200 units.

Below: Driven by Fred Marriott, the Stanley Rocket attained 150 miles per hour (241 km/h) at Ormond Beach in 1907, then hit a ripple in the sand, flew into the air, and was utterly destroyed.

Background: Fred Marriott in the Stanley Rocket.

SPECIFICATIONS

1906 STANLEY ROCKET STEAMER
Top speed: 127.659 mph (205.45 km/h)
Engine: Two double-acting cylinders powered by a vertical fire-tube boiler

Stanley Steamer engines were advertised as having just 13 moving parts, and no transmission, clutch, carburetor, or many of the other components necessary in a gasoline-powered car. The resulting simplicity and trouble-free motoring helped make the Stanley/Locomobile the most popular car in the nation from 1900 to 1904.

Stanleys were also the fastest vehicles of their time. The brothers built their first racing car in 1903. Known alternatively as the Turtle and the Torpedo, the streamlined racer was the first Stanley to set a world speed record for steam-powered cars. F. E. Stanley took second place in the Mount Washington "Climb to the Clouds" race in New Hampshire in both 1904 and 1905. Also, in 1905, a Stanley Steamer set a speed record for the flying mile at Ormond Beach, Florida, which at the time was host to annual land-speed record competitions and races.

In January 1906, driver Fred Marriott piloted the Stanley Rocket to a series of records over several days at Ormond Beach, including the one-mile steam championship and five-mile open races. On January 26, Marriott became the

"Power—Correctly Generated, Correctly Controlled, Correctly Applied to the Rear Axle."

—An early advertising slogan for the Stanley Steamer

first driver ever to exceed two miles in one minute in any vehicle. Two hours later, he and the Rocket set a new world land-speed record at 127.659 miles (205.45 km) per hour. That record stood for four years, especially impressive in an era when speed records were constantly broken because cars were consistently becoming faster and more technologically advanced. This was an age when most roads were dirt, and the average speed for a passenger car was barely faster than a horse and buggy.

Marriott returned to Ormond Beach in 1907 with hopes of breaking his own record, but it was not to be. Shortly after being clocked by F. E. Stanley at 150 miles (241.4 km) per hour, Marriott lost control of the Rocket on the uneven surface of the beach, and the car was smashed to pieces in a spectacular crash. Incredibly, Marriott survived with only a concussion, broken ribs, and some cuts. He vowed to return the following year.

A combination of rule changes banning short-distance steam racers, and the brothers' concern for their driver's safety meant that Stanley Steamers would never again return to Ormond Beach. Fred Marriott did make a full recovery, however, and continued to race Stanleys at other events.

As the brothers lost interest in racing, technological development of their Steamers began to stagnate. Meanwhile, the internal combustion engine was catching up in the marketplace, fueled by developments like the electric starter in 1912 and by Henry Ford's ubiquitous Model T. The Stanleys were never interested in mass-producing their cars, and by 1914, Ford produced as many cars in a single day as the Stanleys did in a year— for a quarter of the price of a Steamer. The brothers sold the Stanley Motor Carriage Company in 1917, and the last Stanley Steamer rolled off the line in 1924.

Below: Best remembered as the pilot of "Old 999," cigar-chomping Oldfield was the first driver to complete a lap at Indy at over 100 miles (161 km) per hour. Here, he poses with his unique "Golden Submarine" race car.

BARNEY OLDFIELD

One of the most recognized names in automobile racing is that of a man who started out competing on bicycles before there were cars to race. The fact that he retired from racing by 1918 only added to his legend.

Barney Oldfield (1878–1946) graduated from bicycles to gas-powered bikes, and in 1902 traveled to Michigan to meet with Henry Ford about driving one of his first race cars. Sadly for Ford, neither of the two examples prepared for Barney's arrival would start. Ford sold both to Oldfield for $800; Oldfield subsequently worked on the cars and then went on to win races and set records in them.

Despite being suspended from racing, because the American Automobile Association considered his speed record attempts "outlaw" behavior, the cigar-chomping Oldfield returned to the racing circuit and competed at the Indianapolis 500 twice. He became the first Indy 500 competitor to complete a lap at over 100 miles (161 km) per hour, though he never actually won at the Brickyard.

STP-Paxton Turbine Car

The Indianapolis 500 is an institution in motor racing, and like all institutions, change comes slowly at Indy. Open-wheel cars have developed in a more evolutionary than revolutionary fashion since the first Indianapolis race of 1911. But once in a while, something comes along to truly shake things up in the world of the Brickyard.

One such shake-up came in 1967, when Andy Granatelli (b. 1923)—holder of more than 400 land-speed records, designer of engines for Chrysler, Cadillac, and Studebaker, and CEO/marketing whiz for engine oil treatment maker STP—unleashed the first turbine-powered Indy car.

Built completely in-house at the Granatelli brothers' shop, far away from any prying eyes, the turbine car was one of the best-kept secrets in racing history when it was introduced to the media before the 1967 race. Designed specifically for Indianapolis, every piece of it, save for the engine, wheels, and tires, is said to have been built at the Granatelli shop. With the driver sitting alongside a 550-horsepower Pratt & Whitney gas turbine engine, both the shape and performance of the car were unlike anything Indy had ever seen.

The lightweight but bulky turbine was positioned on the left side, and the fiberglass skin stretched over it and the driver's compartment to the right, creating an oddly wide and asymmetrical shape compared to other race cars. Four-wheel drive, another unusual

Driver Parnelli Jones, in a white jumpsuit, stands behind the STP-Paxton Turbine Car as racing press, officials, and enthusiasts crowd around prior to the 1967 Indianapolis 500. Although it was plenty fast and furious, the record breaking STP turbine car failed just three laps short of victory. It is now in the collection of the Smithsonian Institution.

feature for the time, combined with the car's light weight, made it especially maneuverable, and it is said that not only could the STP car be competitive high or low on the track, rather than being limited to a more conventional "line," but that it could literally drive around other cars.

When the famous "Gentlemen please start your engines" signaled the start of the 1967 race, driver Parnelli Jones and the turbine car showed their stuff by leading 171 of the race's 200 laps. Then, with

just seven miles to go, a bearing failure brought an end to the turbine's debut, and the car coasted to an unceremonious stop on the track.

Authorities wasted little time changing the rules for 1968, and limited air available for the hard-breathing turbine. Power was reduced to about 480 horsepower—or some 270 horsepower less than conventional piston engine cars. Still, a new STP turbine car developed with British race-car builder Lotus dominated the 1968 Indy, leading until lap 192 when a failed fuel pump shaft sidelined the car, along with Granatelli's—and anybody else's—ambitions for turbine-powered Indy cars.

The STP team stayed with Lotus in 1969, but went with a conventional piston engine driven by Mario Andretti. This time, the car took the checkered flag.

Joe Leonard, in the number 60 Lotus turbine car, leads the field early in the 1968 Indy 500. Despite heady competition with Bobby Unser, Leonard was once again in the lead on lap 192, when the turbine car failed, dropping Leonard out of the race and bringing heartbreak to Andy Granatelli and the STP team for the second year in a row.

SPECIFICATIONS

1967 STP-PAXTON TURBINE CAR
Driver: Parnelli Jones
Final Place: Sixth
Fastest race lap: 54.57 sec at 164.926 mph (265.422 km/h)
Engine: Pratt & Whitney ST6B-62 gas-turbine engine rated at 550 hp

The Little Red Wagon

Drag racing hit the big time in the 1960s, when it evolved from a sort of backyard enterprise into a major motor sport with television coverage, an audience that extended beyond the participants themselves, and the all-important factory sponsorship. Gas was cheap, fast cars were cool, and bands like The Beach Boys were singing about horsepower. You could not even hum along with Jan & Dean's "The Little Old Lady from Pasadena" without learning something about the importance of fast quarter-mile times.

Money flowed freely from Detroit, and manufacturers were big on the "Win on Sunday, sell on Monday" mantra that had started with stock-car racing. As the popularity of muscle cars like the Pontiac GTO grew, carmakers rolled out all kinds of race cars to grab the public and the TV camera's attention.

As it rolled off the assembly line, the Dodge A100 pickup was about as removed from cool as a vehicle could get. With the nose of a van and the body of a pickup, it had neither the swagger nor the cargo capacity of other trucks. Powered by the Chrysler Corporation's legendary 101-horsepower, six-cylinder engine known as the slant six and better remembered for reliability than speed, the

SPECIFICATIONS

LITTLE RED WAGON
(Modified Dodge A100 pickup)
1/4 mile (0.4 km): 10+ sec at 125+ mph (193 km/h)
Longest "wheelie": 4,230 ft (1,289.3 m)
Engine: 426 Hemi V8 rated at 425 hp (313 kw) at 6,000 rpm

A100 was an unlikely candidate for the quarter-mile wars—that is, until Chrysler engineers stuffed a supercharged 426-cubic-inch Hemi V8 and Torqueflite automatic transmission into one example, and The Little Red Wagon was born.

While the stock engine was located alongside the driver and in front of the cargo box, the much larger and four-times-more-powerful Hemi took up part of both, and shifted weight distribution to the rear. To shave pounds and further quicken the truck, engineers removed the front bumper, dashboard, heater, most of the wiring and cab interior except for the body sealer and weather stripping; even the windshield wipers and their motor were scrapped. Steel doors were swapped for fiberglass replacements, and cab glass was replaced with lighter Plexiglas.

This helped quicken the truck, but it also shifted the weight bias further aft. The result was a pickup truck capable of an 11-second quarter-mile, but one that also had an unsettling tendency to raise its front wheels whenever power was applied. The unintended wheelies may have spooked the driver and designers, but the crowds loved it.

Instead of trying to figure out how to keep the Dodge's nose and driver Bill "Maverick" Golden closer to the tarmac, it was decided to exploit this unexpected talent of The Little Red Wagon, and it went on to become one of the most memorable dragsters of the 1960s, thrilling crowds as it hurtled down drag strips at more than 100 miles (161 km) per hour with its front wheels in the air.

This is Bill "Maverick" Golden's original Little Red Wagon, the first wheelstanding dragster ever to compete. Not long after this photo was taken, Golden crashed the truck. Another one was built in due time, and more have followed. Golden still races the Little Red Wagon, and the wheelstander remains a crowd favorite to this very day.

Plymouth Superbird

Homologation is a little regulation in the rulebooks of some forms of racing that says it is okay to run various wings, snouts, engines, and other trick stuff on the track, as long as carmakers build a certain number of similar examples for the street.

The Plymouth Superbird of 1970, along with its sister ship, the Dodge Charger Daytona, introduced in 1969, are two of the more extreme examples of homologation ever built. With an extended, pointed nose intended to provide better aerodynamics than the boxy Plymouth Road Runner, on which it was based, the Superbird also had a huge wing at the rear, roughly as tall as the roof. Intended to help keep the cars planted on the high ovals of NASCAR at the 200-mile- (321.9 km) per-hour speeds race versions were capable of, the wings also gave taller civilian owners a handy place to put groceries while they fumbled with trunk keys. Like the wing, the 19" nose extension made little sense for the street, as it had little effect on aerodynamics at highway speeds. It did, however, make parallel parking a bit dicey.

Not a car for wallflowers, the Superbird was sold in a variety of flamboyant shades, such as lime

SPECIFICATIONS

1970 PLYMOUTH SUPERBIRD
Top speed: 130–160 mph (209–257 km/h)
0–60 mph: 5.5 sec
1/4 mile (0.4 km): 14.26 sec at 103.7 mph
   (167 km/h)
Engine: (optional) 426 Hemi cast iron, 90
   degree V-8 rated at 425 hp (313 kw)
   at 5,000 rpm and 490 lb ft (665 nm)
   of torque at 4,000 rpm

Below: With values approaching half a million dollars today, it is hard to believe that dealers once clipped the wings off of slow-selling Superbirds just to get them off the lot.

Background: Richard Petty's 1970 Road Runner Superbird is on display at the Richard Petty museum in North Carolina.

green, electric blue, and bright orange. A tasteful vinyl roof covering, popular on street cars of the time, was also available. If all this was not enough to stop owners from taking themselves too seriously, the Superbird featured a horn that sounded like the cartoon character Road Runner. It even carried a full-color image of the Road Runner character—holding a racing helmet—on each side of the wing. Interestingly, and possibly due to the added weight of its nose and wing, the Superbird was actually slower in quarter-mile drag racing than a comparably equipped Plymouth Road Runner.

Street models of the Superbird could be purchased new for $4,298, as long as owners were content without the legendary 426-cubic-inch Hemi engine that formed the basis for the race car. A total of 1,920 Superbirds were built for street use, and just 135 of those were equipped with the Hemi. Some were even discounted by dealers after languishing unsold on their lots. Even in the heady days of the Woodstock generation, some things were just too weird. It is said that some dealers, unable to sell them, converted them back to conventional Road Runners. Recently, however, Superbirds equipped with the Hemi have traded for more than $400,000, and prices are still rising.

The Superbird and Daytona were virtually unbeatable on the track, but they were not around for long. Victims of their own success, they brought howls of protest from competitors, and rule changes made them uncompetitive after the 1970 season.

FORD TORINO TALLADEGA

Even before the arrival of the Superbird, Ford knew it needed a more aerodynamic car to be competitive with the Chrysler Hemis on the ovals of NASCAR. So in 1969, a smoothed and extended nose was grafted onto the front of the Torino fastback, creating the Talladega.

Named for the then-new Alabama speedway where it would soon compete, the Talladega's headlights and grille were mounted flush to the front for better airflow, and a rear bumper was reworked to harmonize with the nose.

Like the Superbird and Daytona, homologation rules dictated that Ford build a street version of the car, and approximately 750 Talladegas were built for the public, equipped with a 428-cubic-inch, 335-horsepower engine.

When the dust settled at the end of the season, the longer nose did help make the Fords somewhat more competitive. But it still was not enough to beat the Hemis.

Chaparral 2J

There is a concept in race car design called ground effect, which, in layman's terms, means controlling airflow to maximize

downforce and thus increase traction. It works on a reversal of the Bernoulli effect, best known for keeping airplanes aloft. Just as an airplane wing is designed to provide lift, ground effect manipulates the air passing underneath a car in order to lower the car closer to the ground.

Chaparral Cars was known for designing and building innovative racers. Owner Jim Hall, an oil magnate turned Formula One driver, was obsessive about aerodynamics. His cars often featured sleek bodies and huge wings. One famous Chaparral, the 2C, even had a moving wing over the rear that the driver operated with a foot pedal.

Perhaps the most famous of Jim Hall's creations was the Chaparral 2J. Hall designed the 2J for the Sports Car Club of America's Group 7 Can-Am Racing Series. Designers for other teams had been copying many of Hall's aerodynamic tricks, and by 1968 Hall was looking for an edge. Understanding that wings and spoilers only created downforce when a car was at speed, he wanted to generate downforce at the lower speeds of cornering.

After two years of development, Hall introduced the 2J to stunned race fans. The 2J looked nothing like any other Group 7 racer. Along the sides were two metal skirts that began at the front wheels, obscuring the undercarriage and rear wheels. In the rear were two large, industrial-looking fans. These features did not make for an attractive car, but they were effective.

A 700-horsepower Corvette ZL1 engine powered the 2J. However, it was the two giant fans in the rear that made the car a force with which to be reckoned. The fans sucked air from beneath the car and blew it out the back. This vacuuming created some 1,000 pounds of added downforce, and the skirts helped seal the bottom for additional grip. Powered by their own engine, the fans provided downforce at all speeds.

The 2J was able to take corners at much greater speeds than other Group

"The amazing thing about it was that it didn't rely on aerodynamics so it worked as well on slow corners as it did on fast corners."

—VIC ELFORD, ONE OF THE DRIVERS OF THE CHAPPARAL 2J

7 cars; what would normally be a 40-mile- (64.37 km) per-hour corner became a 50-mile- (80.47 km) per-hour corner for the 2J. And added corner speed meant that the car entered straightaways at greater speeds.

Unfortunately, the Chaparral 2J was not a world-beater, despite posting some of the fastest qualifying times for races in which it competed. For one, it was not an easy car to drive. It generated so much g-force in corners that drivers had a difficult time just keeping their heads upright. Even Hall complained about getting banged up driving the 2J. Also, through the 1970 season, various mechanical problems kept the 2J from being competitive in a number of races.

Still, by season's end, the 2J's potential had many race teams worried. Several petitioned the SCCA to outlaw the 2J's gripping technology, claiming that the car pulled gravel and debris up from the track and hurled it back at following cars. The SCCA agreed and banned the ground-effects technology behind the 2J. It was back to the drawing board for Jim Hall.

Eight years later, the Brabham BT46B Formula One car used a similar technology, but like the 2J, it was banned from Formula One competition soon after.

A master of aerodynamics, Jim Hall created race cars unlike any ever seen before. As strange as the Chaparral 2J looks from the front however, it was the powerful fans in the rear that made the car unique, and eventually unwelcome, at the racetrack.

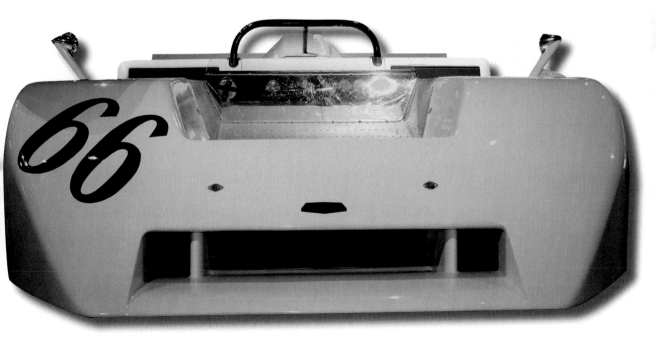

Brabham Alfa BT46B

Designing for maximum ground effect has resulted in some innovative, extremely competitive, and mysterious race cars, because most of what makes it work cannot be seen. Some went on to spectacular wins in their first race, and were subsequently outlawed from further competition right on the spot. One such car was the Brabham Alfa BT46B, designed to race in the 1978 Swedish Grand Prix.

Designer Jim Hall revolutionized the concept of ground effect with his 1970 Chaparral 2J, adding side skirts to seal the car's underside, and a large horizontally mounted fan that literally sucked the car to the ground. Mr. Hall's design worked so well, it was promptly banned from further competition.

When designing the Brabham Alfa BT46B, Formula One designer Gordon Murray borrowed rather creatively from Hall's fan concept. Already familiar with

ground effect from both his and competitors' designs, Murray's big break came when he discovered a loophole in the rules that allowed a fan to be used if its primary function was not to help with aerodynamics, but to help with engine cooling. Murray's design did indeed cool the engine, but the entire engine compartment was also sealed, so surrounding air wouldn't be drawn through it, which would break the seal of the skirts and ground effect.

The result was a competition-crushing car best remembered for a rather conspicuous, rear-mounted engine-cooling fan as tall as the car's body. It enabled the BT46B to stick to the track as if glued to it. It worked so well that when driver Niki Lauda blipped the throttle at standstill, the entire car squatted noticeably closer to the ground. While ostensibly keeping engine temperature under control,

the fan did little to keep the tempers of competitors from overheating, and protests commenced even before the race did.

The car was allowed to race, and Lauda went on to win by a comfortable margin, especially after another race car spilled oil on the track, making the surface especially slick. While competitors struggled to negotiate the slippery surface, the Brabham cruised as if out for a Sunday drive.

When it was over, Niki Lauda and the BT46B had won by 34.6 seconds, an eternity in Formula One racing. In spite of the protests, the win stood, but officials banned the BT46B and its controversial fan from further competition. However, ground effect without mechanical assistance—at least that inspectors are aware of—remains a critical part of race car design to this day.

Above: Three-time Formula One World Champion Niki Lauda is one of the greatest drivers in auto-racing history. He was a victim of a disastrous crash at the 1976 German Grand Prix, becoming trapped in the flaming wreckage of his car, and later falling into a coma. Lauda survived with severe burns to his head and face, and his conspicuous scars became a distinctive feature in the eyes of the public. He returned to racing six weeks later, and returned to form as the 1977 Formula One World Champion.

Left: The Brabham BT46B at the 2001 Goodwood Festival of Speed. The outsized fan is visible on the back of the car.

CHAPTER 3

OTHERWORLDLY CARS

THERE ARE NORMAL CAR DESIGNERS, and then there are those who think outside the box. Then there are those who think way outside the box—even outside the atmosphere. In this chapter, we look at the work of some of these individuals.

While most automobiles are designed to operate on planet Earth's extensive network of roads, others have been intended to cruise oceans and waterways, roam the frozen Arctic tundra, or even fly.

Vehicles like the lunar rover and Mars rover were each designed to operate in the unforgiving environment of space, on celestial bodies under unique and harsh operating conditions, far removed from any mechanic (or at least any mechanic in the Yellow Pages). Both of these crafts are a credit to their designers in that they successfully aided NASA in the ambitious goal of learning more about worlds beyond this planet.

Visionary vehicular design on Earth has enabled humans to explore and learn about some of the most inhospitable parts of the globe, and brought to life the otherworldly automotive dreams of countless enthusiasts, young and old. Hats off to those ingenious designers and engineers. What will they come up with next?

Apollo 17 mission commander Eugene A. Cernan takes a preliminary test drive in the Lunar Roving Vehicle (LRV), prior to loading the vehicle up for an extended foray of the Taurus-Littrow landing site.

Amphibious Cars

Renderings of futuristic amphibious vehicles have long graced the covers of technology magazines such as *Popular Mechanics* and *Popular Science*.

In 1961, a German manufacturer introduced the first mass-produced amphibious car ever, called the Amphicar. Nearly 4,000 were built for sale to the public during its seven-year run. The Amphicar used a slant-4 engine from the Triumph Herald and Saab 99, which produced 43 horsepower, enough to get it to seven knots on smooth seas. Because of its modest

performance on both land and water, the Amphicar was not very successful; the last one was built in 1968.

In spite of the Amphicar's limited success as both a so-so boat and not-particularly good automobile, other

A flotilla of Amphicars gathers on Grand Lake St. Marys, near Celina, Ohio, for the annual convention of the Amphicar Owner's Club.

Well-dressed Sir Richard Branson demonstrates that when you have to get across the English Channel in an hour and a half, there is no more fashionable ride than a Gibbs Aquada.

hobbyists and small manufacturers have continued to unveil amphibious cars over the years. Most were not much more than wheels added to a boat design, or cars modified to be buoyant.

Progress came in 2003, when Gibbs Technologies, a British company, unveiled the Aquada, an amphibious roadster. Created for the sporting driver, it was invented from the ground up to serve as both a boat and a roadster. The Aquada can reach speeds of more than 100 miles (160.93 km) per hour on the road and 30 miles (48.3 km/26.1 knots) per hour on water.

The Aquada is powered by a 175-horsepower, V6 engine with 4-speed automatic transmission. On the water, the engine employs a fully enclosed jet-propulsion system to power the vehicle.

The Aquada has no doors; occupants have to step in over the beltline of the vehicle to enter. It seats three across a single row, with the driver or pilot in the middle. After entering the water by driving down a boat ramp or a gently sloping beach, the driver pushes a button that disengages the wheels, which then retract sideways into the wheel wells.

As part of a 2004 promotional stunt, billionaire adventurer Richard Branson sailed a Gibbs Aquada to France across the English Channel, setting a new record for an amphibious crossing of the channel in 1 hour and 40 minutes.

As of 2007, the Aquada is available only in the United Kingdom and sells for about $260,000, but plans to sell the car in the United States were recently announced.

Gibbs Technologies has ventured into other amphibious projects as well. It has created an all-terrain vehicle that transforms into a Jet Ski on water, known as the Quadski. It has also built prototypes for a Humvee-like amphibious vehicle with military aspirations called the Humdinga.

Hovercrafts

Hovercrafts are amphibious vehicles that ride on a cushion of air created by one or more engine-powered fans. The resulting cushion beneath the vehicle enables a hovercraft to skim across many surfaces, including pavement, swampland, and even the open sea, where they can provide a smoother ride than conventional boats. Early hovercrafts were mostly experimental vehicles developed by the Soviet Union and the United States, prior to and during World War II. At that time, however, practical applications were limited, and few hovercrafts were built.

In the 1950s, using designs from inventor Christopher Cockerell (who first coined the term "hovercraft"), British military researchers began deploying experimental hovercrafts, and in 1959 one Cockerell design became the first to cross the English Channel. It became evident after the channel crossing that hovercraft might be practically used to quickly transport passengers in crossings where slower ferries were normally employed. Not only could a

Below: The SRN1, a prototype hovercraft invented by Sir Christopher Cockerell, nears the English coast after a successful first crossing of the English Channel. Cockerell is aboard, along with a test pilot and two technicians.

Background: An SRN4 Mountbatten Class hovercraft ferry on its last day in service.

hovercraft travel at higher speeds, passengers and cargo could be boarded and unloaded on dry land.

For a short time in 1962, the first hovercraft ferry went into service. A small, buslike vehicle called the Vickers A3 Rhyl-Wallasey hovercraft regularly transported passengers between seaports in Wales on the Irish Sea. Unfortunately, that hovercraft was wrecked in a storm later that year. Despite the short tenure of the Vickers A3, several British manufacturers continued to develop larger and better hovercrafts, and more of them were deployed in the United Kingdom during the next several years.

In 1968, the British Hovercraft Corporation christened their Mountbatten- (or SRN4) class hovercraft, the largest ever produced. The first was christened *Princess Margaret* and carried some 250 passengers and 30 cars. It ran service across the channel from Dover to Bologna, and the crossing took approximately thirty minutes. The largest of the Mountbatten class could carry more than 400 passengers and roughly 60 automobiles at speeds up to 83 knots (96 mph/154 km/h). The Mountbatten-class hovercrafts were considered to be extremely safe except for the one instance when the *Princess Margaret* hit a breakwater in 1985, resulting in the death of four passengers.

The high-speed English Channel Tunnel (or Chunnel) rail service between England and France opened in 1994, signaling the beginning of the end for the hovercraft ferries. Channel service ended in 2000.

Above: A hovercraft glides across a beach on its way to port. Hovercrafts utilize beaches or ramps for seamless docking on land.

Below: The *Princess Margaret* departing from Dover Port, Kent, England. The opening of the English Channel Tunnel signaled the end of the line for the Mountbatten Class hovercraft ferries, which could carry as many as 400 passengers.

Snowcats

Snowcat is a generic term often used to describe tracked vehicles that are designed to travel off-road over deep snow and in icy conditions. Many are used for ski trail grooming, airport runway snow removal, and as search-and-rescue vehicles, but they have also seen duty as personal cold-climate transportation and as Arctic and Antarctic exploration vehicles. Some snowcats have been used in more temperate areas, to travel over peat bogs, marshes, sand dunes, or the soft gravel and earth of mining sites.

Snowcats typically are truck sized, with an enclosed cab insulated against subzero weather. Many utilize complex heating and wiper systems to help keep condensation from forming on windows. Some newer snowcats also use modern glass coatings on their windshields to help shed ice and snow. Their tracks are usually either made of aluminum, steel, or rubber and ride over rubber or metal wheels. Many ride on two parallel tracks, although some use a more complex system of four or more tracks for added agility in deep snow and traversing steep grades.

Among the more well-known, larger snowcats are the American-built Tucker Sno-Cat and the Canadian-made Bombardier Snomobile. Smaller snowcats include the American Kristi Snowcat and the Swedish Aktiv Snow Trac. All have seen duty in various military, exploratory, and work applications, although the Kristi and Aktiv models have been used as personal vehicles as well.

In the dead of winter, passengers are surely happy to be inside this 1968 Snow Trac.

The Snow Trac, built between 1957 and 1981, is still in use all over the world today. Most notably, it was used by NATO forces in Norway during the Cold War and saw duty in Antarctica by explorers of the continent. Modified, open-top versions of the Snow Trac have been used to travel through slick oil fields and on desert sands, since the track design was suitable for many surfaces that would otherwise be inaccessible to wheeled vehicles or heavier, armored tracked vehicles.

Notably smaller than the truck-like Tucker and Bombardier models, the two-seat Snow Trac was originally designed as a winter recreation vehicle by a farm equipment designer named Lars Larsson. Unlike other snowcats, the Snow Trac (also known by the Snow Master and Trac Master) used a steering wheel instead of pull levers to control the tracks. Because it used engines and parts commonly found in European cars such as Volkswagens and Volvos, many of the some 2,500 built are still in use as both work and personal vehicles.

Of the four companies that produced snowcats, only Tucker still builds them today. Tucker's modern Sno-Cat has adopted a more familiar cab, which the company says is designed to be more like a regular pickup truck to inexperienced drivers, with a steering wheel and foot controls for the throttle and brakes.

Above: A 1968 Snow Trac, at home in the elements. Because of their ease of use and commonly available parts, Snow Tracs are still widely used.

Below: A Tucker K23 Sno-Cat perched atop a snow mound. Parking the vehicle on a snow mound helps avoid its being buried in snowdrifts.

Moller M400 Skycar

Ever since Henry Ford predicted "A combination airplane and motorcar is coming," the concept of a flying car has captivated the American psyche. In the many years since Mr. Ford's prediction, flying cars have been a favorite subject of futurists and science-magazine writers, and have been the stuff of dreams for a commuting public growing ever more weary of battling traffic congestion.

Decades ago, the concept also captivated a Canadian-born aeronautical engineer named Paul S. Moller (b. 1937). He has spent close to 40 years trying to develop a four-person vehicle designed to take off and land vertically, and capable of cruising through the skies at speeds approaching 300 miles (482.8 km) per hour.

The prototype that Moller's company has been working on, called the M400, looks much like a flying car from the movie *Blade Runner*. Moller International says it will be powered

by eight lightweight, redundant rotary engines. The company predicts that the finished product will produce a total of 1,000 horsepower and get 20 miles per gallon (8.49 km/l) on ethanol-based fuel.

The M400 would be a car only in the sense that it would be as simple to operate and would not require a pilot's license to fly. The driver would need only input the desired speed and heading, and the Skycar would handle the piloting. A parachute would deploy in case of emergency, and softly guide the vehicle to the ground.

To make the M400 even more accessible to the general public, Moller plans to build it to fit in a typical suburban garage and be able to drive on roads for short distances. Moller has said that his Skycar would eventually be as affordable as a luxury car, although initial units would cost close to $1 million.

To insure investors that the M400's technology was feasible, the company flew a prototype in a tethered test in 2003, and the company plans more flight tests after modifications are completed on an updated prototype. Moller International says that it expects to have FAA certification by the end of 2008, and that the company is taking refundable deposits from individuals interested in buying one.

The 2005 Neiman Marcus Christmas catalog even featured an M400 prototype, but cautioned that it might not be legal to fly. In 2006, Moller International, in need of development capital, auctioned a prototype on eBay and asked for a $3.5 million reserve price. Sadly for Mr. Moller and his 40-year quest, there were no takers.

CARS THAT DRIVE THEMSELVES

Cars that can handle piloting chores and leave drivers to read the paper or take a snooze have long been the dream of sci-fi fans, futurists, and a lot of commuters. They are not here yet, but they may be closer than you think. Cars like Audi's Q7 SUV feature what is called Adaptive Cruise Control, which doesn't just hold a set speed but accelerates and slows with the flow of traffic. While ACC has been around for a few years, the Audi system can even bring the Q7 to a complete stop and get the car underway again as conditions permit, provided traffic starts to move again within a few seconds.

Infiniti has a system that alerts drivers if they start to wander out of their lane, and both Audi and Volvo have systems that monitor other traffic on the road and warn drivers who attempt a lane change that might cause an accident.

Within a few years, expect cars and roads that can communicate with each other to warn of traffic ahead, or other delays. So, relax and grab your coffee and newspaper—it is coming faster than you think.

Lunar Rover

The Lunar Roving Vehicle (aka lunar rover or LRV) of the Apollo Space Program may be the most extreme off-road vehicle ever made. If nothing else, lunar rovers ventured farther off any road than any other vehicle big enough to carry passengers ever has.

A total of four lunar rovers were built, and three of them were sent to the moon on the *Apollo 15*, *16*, and *17* missions. The fourth stayed back on Earth after future Apollo missions were cancelled.

The LRV was first conceptualized by Dr. Wehrner von Braun (1912–77) during the Gemini missions, when the German rocket scientist was director of the Marshall Space Flight Center. Von Braun envisioned a manned vehicle that would enable astronauts to explore areas of the moon they could not reach on foot.

An electric car designed to operate in a low-gravity environment, the lunar rover had to be capable of traversing the barren, rocky, and unpredictable surface of the moon. On earlier Apollo missions, astronauts on foot, slowed by their bulky equipment, could explore only a small area. The rover, with its top speed of about eight miles (12.87 km) per hour, allowed them to travel as far as four miles from the lunar capsule.

Lunar rovers were built by both Boeing and Delco, and cost NASA a total of $38 million. Weighing 463 pounds, each was designed to carry a payload of a little more than 1,000 pounds on the moon's surface. In addition to the four rovers, several training vehicles were also built. Fully loaded, the LRV had a ground clearance of about 14 inches (36 cm), about the same as some modern sport-utility vehicles.

With its thin frame made of aluminum alloy tubing, the LRV was hinged at the middle to hang folded in the lunar module. Its two seats were also aluminum, with nylon webbing covering the seating areas. Both occupants had adjustable footrests and Velcro-secured safety belts. A large dish-shaped communications antenna was mounted high in the front of the vehicle.

Because conventional air-filled pneumatic tires would be of little use in an environment with little gravity and no atmosphere, the Lunar Rover's wheels were made of spun aluminum and its tires were zinc-coated spring-steel wire mesh. Treads made of titanium helped the LRV paddle through the moon dust. Each wheel was powered by its own 186-watt direct-current electric drive. Steering was also electric, with separate motors for the front and rear wheels, which turned in opposite directions (when the front wheels turned left, the

> "The Rover comes with a written, one hundred percent lifetime warranty."
>
> —Astronaut Eugene A. Cernan

SPECIFICATIONS

LUNAR ROVING VEHICLE (LRV)
Top Speed: 8 mph (12.87 km/h)
Total distance traveled:
Apollo 15: 17.25 miles (27.8 km)
Apollo 16: 16.5 miles (26.6 km)
Apollo 17: 22.3 miles (35.9 km)

rear wheels turned right) in order to provide a narrower steering radius. Two 36-volt batteries powered all components of the LRV.

Each rover was used on three exploratory trips, one per day over each three-day lunar mission. A T-shaped controller, which controlled the throttle, steering, and brakes sat between the two seats allowing either astronaut to drive. The astronauts navigated by continuously recording direction and distance using a directional gyroscope and an odometer, linked to an onboard computer. There was also a device that worked much like a sundial, which could give the astronauts a manual heading based on the location of the Sun.

Getting a look at one of the original LRVs would involve a bit of a trip, because each of the three sent to the moon is still there. All were abandoned after their missions. Fortunately, an LRV used by the Apollo astronauts for testing is on display at the National Air and Space Museum in Washington, D.C.

Long before sport utility vehicles became fashionable with Americans, the lunar rover featured all-wheel-drive and went further off-road than most suburbanite adventurers could ever dream of going. Here, the lunar rover from *Apollo 15* sits in its final resting place, photographed by Commander Dave Scott. It is still there to this day, as is the Bible that Commander Scott left sitting between the seats.

Mars Rovers

Remotely controlled vehicles that double as areological (study of the geology of Mars) laboratories have been an integral part of NASA's unmanned exploration of the planet Mars.

The original rover, called *Sojourner*, was part of the Pathfinder space program that reached Mars in July 1997. A small, six-wheeled vehicle, *Sojourner* was only 19 inches high, 26 inches wide, and weighed just 23 pounds. It was electrically powered, drawing its energy from a panel of photovoltaic cells on its top. The diminutive rover looked like a toy built from an erector set—although a mighty expensive one.

Sojourner was released from the *Pathfinder* lander on the second Martian day (called a sol by NASA) after *Pathfinder* reached Mars's surface. It traveled slowly, about two feet per minute, and was able to travel a distance equal to some five football fields away from the lander. NASA's scientists controlled it by sending commands to the *Pathfinder* lander, which relayed them to *Sojourner*.

Sojourner sent 550 photo images back to Earth, and performed soil and rock chemical analyses on 16 locations at the rocky Martian flood plain called Ares Vallis. The lander, in the meantime, took some 16,000 pictures and made millions of atmospheric calculations. The lander lost contact with *Sojourner* after 83 sols, due to electronic failures caused by cold Martian nights. Still, the rover and the lander performed well. Originally

An artist's rendering of a NASA Mars Exploration Rover amid the red dust of Mars. Two such rovers, *Spirit* and *Opportunity*, landed on Mars in January 2004, and are still there, sampling the Martian geology and photographing the rugged landscape.

"We're back. And we're on Mars."

—NASA ADMINISTRATOR SEAN O'KEEFE,

ANNOUNCING THE SUCCESSFUL LANDING OF THE *SPIRIT* ROVER ON MARS

Left: *Opportunity* at work: The image on the left shows the rover's rock abrasion tool before it grinds into a rock. On the right, the tool is coated with red dust after making its abrasion.

Below: The first Mars Rover, named *Sojourner*, was just 19 inches (48 cm) high and weighed roughly 20 pounds (9 kg). It went to work exploring the red planet in 1997. Here, it samples a large Martian rock known as "Yogi."

expected to only last a few weeks, the mission went on for nearly three months.

Buoyed by the success of *Sojourner*, NASA green-lighted a second generation of Mars rovers. The Mars rover mission began in 2003 and sent the larger and more advanced six-wheeled *Spirit* and *Opportunity* rovers to the Martian surface. Their mission was to characterize a wide range of minerals and soils to determine if the surface of Mars might have once held water or sustained life.

The rovers were launched within a month of each other, and landed on opposite sides of Mars, 21 days apart in January 2004. Initial photographs from *Spirit*, which landed first, were broadcast over the Internet from NASA's Web site to an amazingly large audience—NASA recorded some 1.7 billion page hits. In March

2004, excited scientists held a press conference announcing that pictures and data sent back from *Opportunity* hinted at the possibility of liquid, likely water, flowing in a region that the rover was exploring.

In 2007, the twin rovers marked their third-year anniversary on the planet and, despite some small setbacks, both are still functioning and sending data back to Earth (the original mission was slated to last 90 days). NASA, meanwhile, announced plans for a fourth Mars rover, a much larger six-wheeled vehicle that, if built, would reach the Red Planet's surface in 2010.

CHAPTER 4

CARS AND MARKETING

MUCH LIKE THE NOTION that automobile racing has been going on since the second automobile was built, advertisers have been finding ways to capitalize on the appeal of the automobile for a very long time.

Some brands, like Oscar Mayer, have been working the state fairs and parades of America since the 1930s. The Wienermobile has become almost as much of an accompaniment to their hot dogs as are mustard and ketchup.

Other companies have partnered with one another to create a greater impact together than either might have been able to do alone, as Levi's and the now-defunct American Motors did with the faux denim-upholstered Levi's Gremlin of the early 1970s. Levi's survived the partnership, but blue-jean-fabric seats were not enough to save either the Gremlin or American Motors.

Marketers continue to work with car companies, seeking to link their products with the popularity and personality of certain automobiles. Though tried and true standards—rolling billboards and parades, television and movie placements—are still used successfully, internet advertising is increasingly important for brands trying to appeal to young buyers. There is no doubt that the advertising world is already preparing for the opportunities that future developments in automotive technology will bring.

The Oscar Mayer Wienermobile parked at the Minnesota State Fair. There have been eight different generations of Wienermobiles since 1936, giving the wheeled wiener an even longer shelf life than a processed meat product.

Oscar Mayer Wienermobile

One of the best-known and recognized examples of motor vehicle meets marketing is the Oscar Mayer Wienermobile. This could be because there have been Wienermobiles on the roads of America—and at its fairgrounds, festivals, and lots of other places where a hot dog might be sold—since 1936. That is the kind of brand recognition that makes carmakers turn as green as relish with envy. If only Ford, GM, or Chrysler had a model known by seventy years of consumers.

According to the Kraft Foods Web site, the folks now responsible for those wieners, there have actually been eight different generations of Wienermobiles.

And much like models made by major carmakers, each vehicle bearing the Wienermobile name has grown larger and more complex than the one preceding it.

The first Wienermobile was a mere 13 feet long. By the time the 2000 version of the rolling hot dog hit the streets, it had grown to some 27 feet in length and was 11 feet high. Its weight, something all good wiener fans might want to think about, eventually ballooned to more than 10,000 pounds. The latest

Below: Frankly, the 1952 Oscar Mayer Wienermobile does not look all that different from today's model, though it is smaller. This one is on display at the Henry Ford Museum, in Dearborn, Michigan.

Background: There are currently six Wienermobiles traversing America. Here, the "Big Bun" is seen on the highway near Omaha, Nebraska.

model, served up in 2004, boasts voice-activated GPS navigation, a gull-wing entrance door, and an audio center with a wireless microphone—presumably for addressing the Oscar Mayer faithful. Carpeting said to be designed to resemble a frank with everything on it, a description leaving plenty of room for speculation, is also part of the package.

In addition to sporting an ever-increasing waistline, each succeeding Wienermobile has reflected the style of its time. The original was a fairly simple design, with the driver seated in an open cockpit, as was not uncommon at the time. By the time the rockin' fifties rolled around, a considerably longer Wienermobile featured a forward-mounted, glass-enclosed pilothouse, along with a hi-fi sound system—just the thing for those beach barbecues. One of the five originally built in the 1950s is now on display at the Henry Ford Museum in Dearborn, Michigan. By the 1970s, Wienermobiles were adventurously voyaging beyond U.S. borders, and in the 1980s, the now familiar cab-forward design sported period-correct square headlights.

Along with the full-size Wienermobiles, there have been many toy models, pedal cars, plush toys, banks, and even Christmas-tree ornaments. Wienerwhistles, collectibles in their own right, have been handed out

by Wienermobile drivers for years.

The hot dogs may look much the same as they did in 1936, but the Wienermobile changes with the times. Maybe you really can teach an old dog new tricks.

LUER QUALITY MEAT ROCKET

In the rolling hot-dog promotional wars, Oscar Mayer's Wienermobile may get all the glory, but southern California–based Luer Meats had the funnier name with their Luer Quality Meat Rocket. And the bigger meatmobile.

Like the Wienermobile, the Meat Rocket did parade duty in the 1950s and presumably blasted into a state fair or supermarket opening or two. Unlike the Wienermobile, the Meat Rocket wasn't meant to look like a hot dog, although it could be argued that its paint job and overall shape might put parade goers in the mood for a frank. At least that's probably what the people at Luer were hoping.

Also unlike the self-propelled Wienermobile, the Meat Rocket was built on a 35-foot semitrailer, and is said to have weighed some 10,000 pounds (4,536 kg). As the story goes, visitors could actually go inside the rocket, where a projector showed cartoons for the kids that were riddled with ads for, well, you guessed it.

The Luer Quality Meat Rocket may still exist. Rumored to be in Prescott, Arizona, it has been said to be in a junkyard, an amusement park, and in somebody's backyard. Just don't ask Luer Quality meats. An Internet search turned up no sign of the company.

Zippo Chrysler

As a child, Zippo cigarette-lighter inventor George C. Blaisdell had been greatly impressed by the 1918 Pep-O-Mint Life Savers truck, which looked like a giant roll of candy. So when he felt the need to give his windproof lighters a distinctive promotional push, it was only natural for him to build a unique rolling advertisement for his company.

He chose to customize a 1947 Chrysler Saratoga, outfitting it with a pair of giant Zippo lighter replicas in place of the stock passenger cabin. After all, what better way to emphasize the windproof capabilities of a Zippo than by strapping a couple of giant ones to a moving car? Complete with striker wheels and simulated neon flame arcing out of the tops of the lighters, the Chrysler was also festooned with the company name across the front grille and on the Chrysler's hubcaps. It was then sent out to tour the country for several years, making appearances at numerous parades, fairs, trade shows, and other events.

The only problem was, the custom bodywork added considerable weight to the vehicle. More, in fact, than its tires could bear. The Zippo Car became almost as famous across the heartland for blowouts as for public appearances.

In the late 1950s, in order to finally address the tire problem, Zippo brought the Chrysler to a Ford dealer in Pittsburgh, where the plan was to install a truck chassis in place of the Zippo Car's passenger car frame. The Chrysler was disassembled in preparation for the rebuild, only to have the job put on indefinite hold. It seemed that the truck frame would raise the car's height by six inches, which would make it taller than legal for a vehicle of its type—especially one with giant lighters on top. To make matters worse, the $40,000 cost estimate to complete the job apparently did not include further modifications to lower it back down to legal height once the truck frame was installed.

Blaisdell's enthusiasm for the project faded, and the Zippo Car reportedly languished unfinished and presumably frameless at the Ford dealer for years. In the early 1970s, the company decided it wanted its car back, but by then the Ford dealership had closed and the Zippo Car had disappeared.

Zippo ended up purchasing a second 1947 Chrysler in 1996, and promptly set about restoring it to create a second Zippo Car, just like the first one—but more lightweight and equipped with a modern 350-cubic-inch Chevrolet V8. The new Zippo Chrysler was ready for the road in 1997, just in time to commemorate the

50th anniversary of the first.

To this day, the fate of the original Zippo Chrysler is unknown, at least to anybody who is talking. It may still be out there somewhere, but one would think it would be sort of hard to conceal if it was. Still, if you happen to stumble across it in some field or stashed in a barn in the countryside, the folks at Zippo would love to hear about it. The Bradford, Pennsylvania–based company is still in business, even if their first Zippo Car is not.

The new Zippo Chrysler making an appearance at the historic Watkins Glen racetrack in New York State. The new Zippo Chrysler hit the road in 1997, 50 years after the original model debuted.

Hertz Shelby Mustang GT350-H

Few people in the automobile business can hold a candle to Carroll Shelby when it comes to marketing their businesses and themselves. The former chicken farmer from Texas had a long and checkered racing history in venues from Bonneville to Le Mans. When his health forced him to retire from racing in 1960, he turned his attention to design. In this way, Mr. Shelby began a tidy little business based on stuffing Ford V8s into British AC Bristol sports cars and reselling them in the United States as Shelby Cobras.

When the Ford Mustang was introduced in 1964, it was a huge sales hit, a sellout across the country. Looking ahead, Ford wanted to improve its image as a serious performance and competition car to further boost sales for the 1965 model year. Ford

When it was new, this Shelby Mustang could be rented for $17.00 a day and 17 cents per mile from Hertz. Now, expect to pay as much as $200,000 to buy one. And prices are going up.

SPECIFICATIONS

1966 HERTZ SHELBY MUSTANG GT350-H
Top speed: 137 mph (220 km/h)
Engine: V8 rated at 306 hp (228 kw)
@ 6,000 rpm and 329 lb ft (446 nm)
of torque at 4,200 rpm

turned to Shelby, who began converting Mustang fastbacks into Shelby GT350s, with a modified engine, suspension, brakes, and cosmetic details including two distinctive racing stripes. The relationship proved mutually beneficial; the success of GT350s at the track boosted Mustang sales, and bolstered Shelby's business as well.

Shelby's next collaboration came when he teamed up with Hertz car rental to build a run of special GT350s done up in Hertz colors, black with gold stripes, and designated GT350-H. The Hertz Sports

Car Club had been set up for well-heeled travelers, and the exclusive GT350 was a natural for the program. It has been said that Mr. Shelby was not expecting much when he approached Hertz, but he left with an order for 200 cars, upped to 1,000 a month later. Hertz paid about $3,800 for each of the cars, the majority of which were equipped with automatic transmissions. In addition to the black paint scheme, about 50 cars each were built in green, blue, red, and white.

Urban legend is full of stories of Hertz Shelbys being rented for the weekend, only to be returned to Hertz with more pedestrian Mustang V8s in the place of the 306-horsepower Shelby motor. There are also tales of the rent-a-racers being turned in with holes in the floor where a roll cage had been bolted in for a weekend at race courses, where more competitive renters could maybe recoup some of the $17-per-day, 17 cents-per-mile rental cost.

Shelbys are some of the most sought-after of all Mustangs by collectors, and the GT350-H is considered by some to be the cream of the crop. Some examples have sold for over $200,000 recently, not bad for an automobile based on a humble pony car that originally sold for about $3,000.

The legend of the Hertz Shelbys is so strong that the car rental company recently commissioned another run of black-and-gold Shelby Mustangs based on Ford's retro Mustang GT. Available for rent in selected markets like Las Vegas, Hawaii, and Miami, expect to pay more than the old $17 a day if you would like to try one. Or wait until Hertz puts them up for sale—chances are, they will be a good investment.

In 2006, Ford, Shelby, and Hertz collaborated once again to bring a high-performance "rent-a-racer" to the public. The Shelby GT-H Mustang pays homage to the original GT350-H by retaining the black and gold color scheme. However, competitive types should be warned: Hertz is apparently taking measures to ensure that the cars will not be raced.

Hurst/Oldsmobile

In the heyday of the American muscle car, Hurst shifters were the preferred method of shifting gears for drag racers and enthusiasts alike. Needless to say, George Hurst, founder of Hurst Performance Incorporated, had one in his 1968 Oldsmobile 4-4-2. Like many individuals involved in the performance parts industry, George's enthusiasm extended beyond the business, and he was always looking for ways to make his 4-4-2 faster.

One problem was that the 4-4-2, like all General Motors mid-sized performance cars of the 1960s, was not available with an engine larger than 400 cubic inches. GM's policy dictated that their larger engines were only available in their largest models.

George went out and got himself an Oldsmobile 455 engine, and dropped it into his 4-4-2. He found the job was actually not very difficult, and that in addition to providing more power, the

SPECIFICATIONS

1969 HURST/OLDSMOBILE
0–60 mph: 5.9 sec
1/4 mile (0.4 km): 14.03 sec at 101 mph (163 km/h)
Engine: OHV V8 rated at 380 hp (283 kw)
 at 5,000 rpm and 500 lb ft (677 nm) of torque at
 3,200 rpm

455 was lighter than the 400 it replaced. The Hurst/Oldsmobile was born.

A production run of 500 cars was planned late in the 1968 model year, with the conversion being handled by a Michigan shop commissioned to do all 515 in about 30 days. In addition to the engine transplant, the cars got a unique silver paint job with black stripes, special interior trim, and of course, a Hurst shifter. Ram air induction with twin scoops under the front bumper and various tweaks to the engine increased power output to 390 horsepower.

A 1969 Hurst/Oldsmobile, clad in distinctive white and gold. Production of the "Gentleman's Musclecar" started and stopped five times between 1968 and 1988. All in all, some 16,000 Hurst/Oldsmobiles were built, in a variety of styles.

The initial run of cars quickly sold out, and production was even increased by 15 units to appease one dealer pleading for more cars. The Hurst/Oldsmobile was here to stay.

For 1969, the paint scheme was changed to the white-and-gold combination more familiar to fans of the limited-production muscle car. The 1968 model was rather subdued, but the 1969 model had far more in-your-face styling. A large wing spoiler was mounted over the trunk, and the air intakes were relocated to a fiberglass hood with two giant scoops. Available with a 380-horsepower engine, stock 1969 Hurst/Oldsmobiles were said to be capable of 13-second quarter-mile times. With nearly twice as many 1969 models built as in 1968, the 1969 model remains the most distinctive and probably most remembered of all versions. Today, the Hurst Web site prominently features a '69 on its homepage.

Between 1968 and 1988, various versions of the Hurst/Olds were built on and off, with production starting and stopping five times—which could possibly be some kind of record. A total of just under 16,000 were made, including two-door hardtops, convertibles, and even a handful of station wagons built as support vehicles for the Indianapolis 500, where Hurst/Oldsmobiles served as pace cars in 1972 and 1974.

Today, all are collectible, but if you happen to see one of those station wagons, you are looking at a rare bird indeed.

THE QUEEN OF TROPHY QUEENS

Linda Vaughn has been known by many different titles, including First Lady of Drag Racing, and The Race Queen, but she is best known as Miss Hurst Golden Shifter.

Although the blonde Georgia native's career only included a brief and undistinguished stint behind the wheel, she remains one of the most recognizable faces from the racing scene of the 1960s and '70s.

Vaughn's career began in the early 1960s, when she won a beauty pageant at the Atlanta Raceway. Her career truly took off, however, when she caught the eye of George Hurst in 1965. In her miniskirt and white go-go boots, Vaughn was a popular sight at various racing events, representing the company known for the Hurst shifters by parading down the track while posing with a 12-foot-tall, trunk-mounted replica of a shift lever.

Vaughn became so popular that she toured Vietnam to entertain American troops. She was eventually requested at so many events stateside that Hurst had to hire look-alikes, known at the "Hurstettes." In the 1970s and '80s she appeared in the racing movies *The Gumball Rally* and *Stroker Ace*.

Although she gave up her title as Miss Hurst Golden Shifter in the 1980s, Vaughn still serves as a goodwill ambassador to the racing and automotive aftermarket communities.

Levi's AMC Gremlin

By the time the new 1970 models hit showrooms in the fall of 1969, Japanese manufacturers had become a threat to Detroit's big three automakers. Americans developed a taste for smaller cars in the 1960s, and Toyota and Datsun (now Nissan) had demonstrated that imported cars could be reliable and have mainstream appeal. Foreign cars—and some of their buyers—were no longer the butts of as many jokes as they had been.

Domestic car companies scrambled to enter the small-car market, and American Motors won the prize for getting there first. The AMC Gremlin was introduced as a 1970 model, months ahead of the competing Ford Pinto and Chevrolet Vega, which did not arrive until the 1971 model year. In retrospect, maybe Ford and Chevy should have taken another year or two to work on their projects, but that is another story.

Beyond making it to the marketplace first, the Gremlin had little going for it. Essentially a larger sedan chopped off just behind the rear seat, it looked like a hatchet job right from the factory. It also got a six-cylinder engine from the AMC Hornet, on which it was based, which kind of defeated the purpose of going small. Without the gas mileage advantage of the four-cylinder competition, there

In the 1970s, Levi's jeans were cool. The AMC Gremlin was not. Sadly for AMC, neither was a Gremlin with faux-denim seats and Levi's tags. However, these days, the Levi's models are the most valued Gremlins by collectors.

"Levi's Gremlin. The economy car that wears the pants."

—FROM A VINTAGE ADVERTISEMENT FOR THE LEVI'S AMC GREMLIN

was not much of a point to buying a chopped-off sedan, especially one with such clumsy handling.

Never a huge sales success, the Gremlin needed help shortly after its introduction. AMC was failing, and the fact that its products were generally regarded as suitable transportation only for grandparents and pocket-protected individuals did not help matters. Blue jeans, on the other hand, were entirely cool with the Woodstock generation. Enter Levi Strauss & Company.

The Levi's Gremlin was introduced for the 1973 model year, featuring fabric made to look like denim covering the seats, door panels, and map pockets. Levi's distinc-tive copper rivets were fastened to the seats and orange stitching held it all together. Just to ensure that everybody knew this was not your grandfather's Gremlin, a Levi's tag was affixed to each of the front fenders. Unfortunately, that was about all Levi's could do. The handling, styling, and performance were as riveting as any other Gremlin, and production ended by the mid-1970s.

Like many cars of the 1970s, because of poor construction quality and styling that leaves most collectors uninspired, of the few Gremlins that have survived to the new millennium, the most sought-after ones have the Levi's badge. Keep an eye out for it at the auction.

Below: Equipped with an ejector seat and telescoping wheel hubs that could chew up the fenders of other cars, 007's stylish, yet deadly Aston Martin DB5 was the quintessential Bond accessory.

JAMES BOND, CAR SALESMAN

Product placement, where companies happily pay a fee and supply their product in exchange for the exposure a hit film or TV show can provide, has been around for years. There is a reason sitcom stars going back to the 1950s have always driven a new model of the same car year after year.

No one on the large or small screen has driven sales quite like Commander James Bond, who has both shaken and stirred up car sales since his Aston-Martin DB5–driving *Goldfinger* days in the early 1960s. In 1974's *The Man with the Golden Gun*, set in Thailand, Bond, the bad guys, and even the cops drove American Motors' cars—which were never actually sold there.

Goldeneye was released in 1995, just as BMW was launching its new Z3 sports car. Bond got one of the first models, and helped make the Z3 a sales success—especially the blue ones, which was the color of the car he drove in the film.

CHAPTER 5

GROUNDBREAKING AUTOMOBILES

OF THE UNTOLD NUMBERS of cars that automakers have offered to the buying public since the dawn of the automobile business, most were destined to fade into obscurity after their 15 minutes—or 15 years—of fame.

Others were perfectly good designs that provided buyers with reliable and safe transportation for a number of years, but nothing made them particularly memorable.

Some cars, though, changed the automotive landscape forever. Whether it was the way they were built, the technology used in their construction, their innovations in performance, comfort, safety, durability, or some other design element, these cars left a lasting legacy. The Citroën Traction Avant, for example, offered front-wheel drive, an independent front suspension, and unibody construction in the 1930s. Cutting-edge at the time, these innovations are common today.

Not all of these groundbreaking cars were sales successes. Some were simply too far ahead of their time. Others were experimental, and not intended to sell in large numbers to begin with. A few, however, stayed in production for decades and were sold all over the world. These cars were often the work of visionaries who helped improve the motoring world, and whose designs changed the way cars have been made ever since.

Left: This 1926 Model T roadster is one of some 15 million built between 1908 and 1927, making the "Tin Lizzie" the second most popular automobile in history. Only the VW Beetle did better in worldwide sales, and it took it about 50 years to do it. This car is now in the collection of the Smithsonian Institution. Inset: This 1964 Mini Cooper S won the 1965 Monte Carlo Rally. With lightweight and agile handling, the Mini caught the interest of enthusiasts and racers Alec Issigonis never targeted with his design.

Ford Model T

There seems to be an unwritten rule that a book about cars must include the ubiquitous Ford Model T, or "Tin Lizzie." Without question, Henry Ford's (1863–1947) first major-league effort did more than put America on wheels. It changed the world—for better or worse.

The idea was to build a car that the masses could afford, and make it simple, reliable, and durable. Before the Model T, cars were basically built by hand, by any number of small manufacturers scattered around the country and the world. Often, one shop built engines and chassis, and an entirely different shop constructed bodies, which helped keep automobiles out of the reach of all but the wealthiest buyers. Henry Ford aimed to change all

SPECIFICATIONS

FORD MODEL T
Top speed: 45 mph (72 km/h)
Engine: 2.9 liter, four-cylinder engine rated at 20 hp (15 kw) at 1,600 rpm, and 65 lb ft (88 nm) of torque at 1,600 rpm

that by introducing mass production, which was presumably more efficient and cost-effective, to the automotive world.

His plan worked, and some 15 million Model Ts were sold between 1908 and 1927, more than any other car except the original Volkswagen Beetle. By 1909, a Ford catalog reported that Model Ts had been shipped to every state in the Union, along with all European countries, and to distant locations in Asia, Africa, and Australia.

The Model T broke design ground by using a flexible three-point suspension, which helped it weather the rough roads of the time. It also incorporated chrome vanadium steel, an alloy that increased strength while keeping weight down. However, it was the way the Model T was built that truly revolutionized the automobile business. As the first car built on a moving assembly line, it not only dramatically reduced production costs, but also provided Mr. Ford with a ready pool of buyers working at his own rapidly expanding factories.

To sum it up, from any and every angle, there is only one reason why the Ford car so far outsells all other cars:

IT IS A BETTER CAR

Simplicity in Operation

The Ford car must be judged independently of its price. It is astonishingly low in price—and surprisingly high in value

Few changes were made to the Model T during its long run, which helped keep costs down and manufacturing efficiencies up. A variety of body styles were offered over the years, from roadsters and coupes to sedans and trucks. All were built using basically the same chassis and four-cylinder engine with 20 well-intentioned, if not exactly breathtaking, horsepower.

A runaway success with everyone from families buying their first car, to traveling salesmen, to farmers who worked with Model Ts in the fields, the Tin Lizzie became its own rolling advertisement. By 1914, Ford dropped most of its national advertising, and by 1917 the company saw no need to place ads. That was probably a wise decision, because by 1918, Model Ts amounted to half of all American car sales, and the Ford Motor Company was earning more money than all other carmakers combined.

Ford started advertising again in 1923, as competition started heating up

and more modern alternatives became available. Quite possibly a victim of the revolution it had ignited in the automobile business, Ford was losing ground to other manufacturers utilizing mass production to create cars with more style, speed, and comfort. In spite of price cuts and cosmetic upgrades, the basic utility of Ford's aging design was losing appeal to an increasingly fickle and affluent buying public.

By 1927, the Model T rolled into the history books, where it will always have a place. And thanks to its simplicity, durability, and the sheer numbers built, they can still be seen puttering along at the hands of enthusiasts.

By the time this 1923 coupe was built, the Model T was facing increasing competition from rival automakers, though it was still a strong seller and would remain in production until 1927.

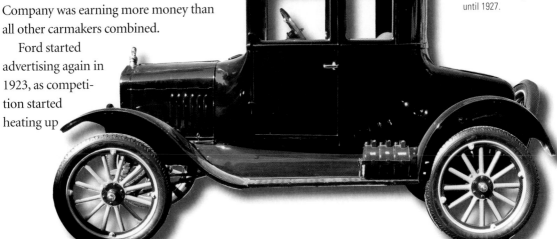

Chrysler Airflow

Nov. 19, 1935.   C. BREER   Des. 97,574
AUTOMOBILE
Original Filed Dec. 13, 1933

Fig. 1.

Fig. 2.

INVENTOR
CARL BREER
Fig. 3. BY
Hanson, Lind, Pitsche Hanne
ATTORNEYS.

Engineer Carl Breer considered his Airflow design so revolutionary, he chose to patent it. Even the "Fig. 1" lettering on Breer's patented design looked aerodynamic.

The idea of designing automobiles to more easily and efficiently slip through the air was just beginning to dawn on most designers in the late 1920s. At the time, car bodies were basically an assemblage of boxes—one for the engine, one for the passengers, and one for the trunk.

In fairness to these designers, streamlining would not have been much of a priority. Poor road conditions and low-powered automobiles made aerodynamics somewhat pointless. Just making a car that would reliably run was hard enough, but—as road conditions improved and consumer demand for higher speeds increased—the idea of smoother shapes for automobiles began to make sense.

A Chrysler engineer by the name of Carl Breer (1883–1970) started thinking about more efficient shapes while watching airplanes and birds. It struck him how brick-like car shapes looked when compared to the sleeker aircraft of the time. With the blessing of Walter P. Chrysler (1875–1940) himself, Breer began looking into applying the same logic to cars.

Working with aviation pioneer Orville Wright (1871–1948), Breer began early wind-tunnel testing of automotive designs, which led to the construction of a wind tunnel at Chrysler's facility in Highland Park, Michigan. When he discovered that cars of the time were actually more aerodynamic going in reverse than forward, Breer had his work cut out for him.

In addition to the brick-like front ends common in cars at the time, abrupt rear-ends were a major impediment to air flow. Designing the Chrysler Airflow, Breer created a smooth, tapered tail and angled both the windshield and the front grille. He incorporated the headlights into the fenders instead of mounting them on top, as was customary at the time.

The Airflow was also constructed with an all-steel unibody, as found in most new car designs today. At the time, wood was still commonly used as part of a car's structure and heavy ladder frames were the norm, but the steel unibody was increasingly prevalent, and the Airflow's use of one placed it at the cutting edge.

One of the design changes dictated by the smoother, tapered rear section of the Airflow was moving both the passenger compartment and the engine forward. This resulted in a comfortable, spacious cabin. Car designs of the period typically positioned rear-seat passengers directly above the rear axle, where they felt every bump. Moving the engine forward placed passengers in front of the rear wheels, and put some engine weight ahead of the front axle, allowing for better weight distribution and more interior room. This has also become standard design practice today.

Although the Airflow created a genuine sensation at its New York Auto Show debut in 1934, like many new designs, it may have arrived before the public was ready for it. Some thought it ugly, and early examples were plagued with quality problems.

Wisely, Walter P. Chrysler had not put all of his eggs in the Airflow basket; the company continued to build more traditional models even after the Airflow's introduction, and these cars remained more popular with the public.

Though Chrysler pulled the plug on the Airflow after the 1937 model year, Carl Breer's legacy lives on. The Airflow remains a groundbreaking design that helped change car design and manufacturing forever.

This 1935 Airflow featured a redesigned grille. Chrysler built its first wind tunnel during development of the Airflow, only to discover that cars of the period cut through the wind better in reverse than going forward.

Cord 810

At a time when most American automobiles were conservatively styled and engineered, the Cord 810 looked like a car from the future. With hidden headlights, exposed exhaust pipes, and a stance so low that it had no need for the era's ubiquitous running boards (which enabled well-dressed passengers to easily step in and out), the 810 was nothing if not distinctive. If its radical styling was not enough of an attention-grabber, color choices including yellows and pinks, when many sedans were still basic black, did the trick.

Errett Lobban Cord (1884–1974) was already a successful businessman when he introduced the 810 to a wowed audience at the 1935 New York Auto Show. At the ripe old age of 33, Cord had founded a holding company specializing in transportation-related businesses. The Cord Corporation owned many well-known brands,

including Duesenberg automobiles, Lycoming (best known for making aircraft engines), and American Airways, which would later become American Airlines. The Cord Corporation also owned Auburn, known as a builder of upmarket cars, and it was Auburn that built the 810.

Nearly a foot lower than other cars of its era, the 810's unusually squat design was possible in part because the transmission was mounted on the front of the engine, rather than behind it (as was and still is the standard for cars with engines mounted lengthwise). The lack of a large transmission tunnel underneath the cockpit allowed for a lower seating area. Also, instead of the upright grille common in cars of the 1930s, the Cord had a rounded nose with horizontal bars wrapping around its sides, making the body look even lower and sleeker. Supercharged V8 models bore trademark chrome

The sleek Cord 810 featured hidden headlights, had no running boards, and was nearly a foot lower than other cars of its time.

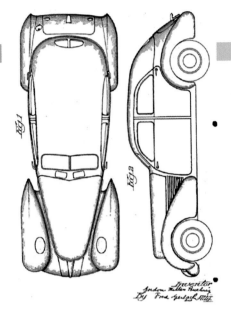

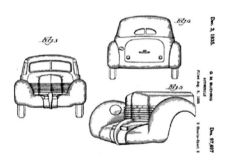

Cord did not have the resources to fully develop their innovative designs, and most Americans could not afford them anyway, in the days of the Great Depression. Early models were plagued with transmissions that popped out of gear, and vapor-lock problems that made winter starting difficult. By the time these were addressed, the damage had been done, and sales of the 810—which cost as much as $500 more than a competing Cadillac of the time—never really took off. After a sad end to a design that was such a sensation right out of the box, E. L. Cord sold his interest in the Cord Corporation in 1937. Much as it goes with mergers and acquisitions today, the company was parceled out and its less profitable products, the 810 among them, ceased to exist.

Unlike so many entrepreneurs who ended up destitute after their automotive dreams died, E. L. Cord went on to become a real-estate magnate and politician in California and Nevada. One can only wonder what he drove around on his business ventures.

Left: These are the signed drawings that Gordon Buehrig submitted for a U.S. patent on his unique 810 design. The retractable headlamps had been patented beforehand, and the 810 was the first car in history to incorporate them.

exhaust pipes, which emerged from the sides of the hood. Admirers were well advised not to touch them when the engine was warm.

It is often speculated that the 810 was simply too far ahead of its time to be accepted by the buying public, but that is probably not what killed it off. After rave reviews and thousands of orders placed at car shows, it seems that the 810 may have been rushed into production before it was ready for prime time. Financially strapped

Below: Though the 810 inspired instant acclaim upon its debut, it was unable to survive as a production model.

Citroën Traction Avant

French carmaker Citroën has long been known for innovation, if—unfortunately for the automaker and buyers of its products—not for altogether reliable cars. Nevertheless, Citroën's engineers can be credited with having produced some groundbreaking designs.

The Traction Avant of 1934–57 is one of those designs. With unibody construction, front-wheel drive, and a body that sat several inches lower than those of its contemporaries, the Traction Avant was way ahead of its time. In addition, the Type 7, as it is also known, featured a revolutionary, independent torsion bar front suspension, hydraulic brakes, and rubber engine mounts to help isolate engine vibration. Though all of these techniques are standard issue for cars of today, this was truly forward-thinking design in

SPECIFICATIONS

1951 TRACTION AVANT SALOON
Top speed: 75 mph (120.7 km/h)
Engine: 1.9 liter, four-cylinder engine rated
   at 56 hp (41.2 kw) at 4,000 rpm

1934. Development of the Traction was so complicated and expensive that it drained company founder André Citroën (1878–1935) financially. The company was taken over by tire maker Michelin in 1935, and André died the same year.

Thanks to the Traction's low center of gravity and advanced suspension design, its handling and road hold-

With front-wheel drive, unibody construction, and a low profile, the Traction was way ahead of its time. Its handling was so good, it became a favorite of the French resistance during WWII.

ing were also far better than other cars of its time—so good, in fact that Tractions became the transportation of choice for the French Resistance during World War II. It is said that few prewar Tractions exist because most were lost in the war effort.

One of the first European cars to be built on an assembly line, early models were equipped with a 1,303 cubic-centimeter (79.5 cu. inch), four-cylinder engine, which later grew to 1,629 cc (99.4 cu. inches) and 1,911 cc (116.6 cu. inches). A V8-powered Traction was shown at the 1934 Paris Motor Show, but this model never reached production, and none of the prototypes are believed to still exist.

Although revolutionary, the Traction was quirky. Early models were built with trunks accessible only from inside the passenger compartment, a feature that was dropped in favor of a more practical and conventional trunk lid in 1936. Various body styles were offered during its 23-year run, including sedans, coupes, cabriolets, and even the eight-passenger Familiale, for large families. Although production was suspended during the war, Tractions began rolling off the line shortly thereafter, and continued their run until long after their sell-by date for maximum freshness, though they remain a tribute to visionary designer Flaminio

Bertoni (1903–64) and chief engineer André Lefèbvre (1894–1963).

Later models were the first to be equipped with Citroën's trademark self-leveling hydraulic suspension, which became standard on the DS model that followed. While Americans do not generally remember Citroëns for trouble-free motoring—it was largely reliability issues that forced the carmaker to withdraw from the U.S. market in the 1970s—Tractions are known for their durability. In 1935, one was driven for a record 250,000 miles in one year by one M. Lecot—clearly a man not only fond of his Traction, but a guy with plenty of time on his hands.

Above: The interior of the Traction seems comfy enough.

Background: It was not until 1936 that the Traction had a trunk lid. Buyers of earlier models had to toss their gear over the back seat.

Mercedes-Benz 300SL Gullwing Coupe

P rior to World War II, Mercedes-Benz enjoyed considerable racing success and benefited from the sales and technological development that racing wins can bring. As the carmaker resumed production following World War II, a return to motor sport was made a priority.

The 300SL was Mercedes-Benz's first postwar competition car, and its racing history was nothing if not impressive. In 1952, 300SL coupes finished first, second, and third at the Grand Prix de Berne in Switzerland, and SLs went on to a one-two finish at the 24 Hours of Le Mans. They also finished in the top three positions at Germany's legendary Nürburgring, where, to this day, manufacturers from around the world bring new designs for high-speed preproduction testing. Together, these and other victories marked

Mercedes-Benz executives had to be convinced to build the Gullwing, a vehicle widely credited with helping establish the carmaker's reputation with American customers as a builder of both well-engineered and high-performance automobiles.

SPECIFICATIONS

1955 MERCEDES-BENZ 300SL GULLWING
Top speed: 160 mph (258 km/h)
0–60 mph (0–97 km/h): 8.8 sec
Engine: 3.0 liter, fuel-injected, straight six-cylinder engine rated at 215 hp (160.3 kw) at 5,800 rpm and 220 lb ft (298.3 nm) of torque at 4,800 rpm

a spectacular return to racing for the legendary German automaker.

Max Hoffman was an importer of European brands to the United States in the 1950s, when demand for imports was growing strong and manufacturers were trying to figure out how best to tap into the American marketplace.

Hoffman not only had the good sense and/or luck to get into the import market at the right time, he had a knack for knowing what models would succeed in America. One of the brands he imported was Mercedes-Benz, and company officials reluctantly listened when he suggested building a street version of the 300SL racing coupe. It is probably a good thing that Mercedes management in Germany paid attention.

The 300SL Gullwing that Hoffman had urged Mercedes-Benz to build was introduced at the New York Auto Show in 1954, where the car was an immediate sensation. It helped establish Mercedes's reputation for both durability and performance with the American public.

The hood, doors, and trunk were constructed of aluminum, although buyers had the option of ordering the entire body in aluminum to save weight. Only 29 buyers opted for this lighter version, and those cars are some of the most sought after today.

Earning its nickname from its doors, which were hinged at the roof and resembled a bird's outstretched wings when opened, the Gullwing's body was built over a lightweight, strong tubular chassis designed for the race circuit. The frame weighed just 110 pounds. The doors were hinged at the top because the frame rails passed through the middle section of the body, where a conventional door would normally open. To enter the car, the driver and passenger would lift the doors, sit on the wide sill, and slide into the cockpit. The steering wheel was designed to fold out of the way, in order to facilitate entry. Once inside, a comfortable and functional, if not overly luxurious cockpit greeted those who went through the gymnastics required to get in.

Powered by a 3.0-liter, six-cylinder engine that produced 215 horsepower, the Gullwing was the first production car to use fuel injection. Its light weight helped it attain a top speed of 160 miles (258 km) per hour.

Just 1,400 road cars were built before production ended in 1957. Their low production numbers, racing pedigree, distinctive shape, and beautiful, streamlined styling combine to make Gullwings some of the most desirable and expensive Mercedes-Benz models for today's collectors. One recently sold for $451,000 at auction. If you can find one of the all-aluminum models, expect to pay considerably more.

The interior of the Gullwing is tricky to enter, and is smaller than it appears through the tall doorway. The lightweight frame of the Gullwing necessitated its trademark doors—frame rails run just beneath the high doorsills.

Volvo 122

Although not especially notable in other respects, the 122 introduced the world to the three-point shoulder harness, often credited with saving more lives than any other piece of safety equipment.

Safety was not much of a priority for either carmakers or buyers in the heady and optimistic days of 1950s' America. Prosperity was up, gas was cheap, and longer, lower, and wider models, with ever increasing horsepower, greeted the public every fall. In short, automotive life was good. Though the need for auto safety standards had begun to become apparent due to new efforts at scientific crash testing, both motorists and manufacturers chose to focus on performance and styling. In the words of one Alfred E. Neuman, a cartoon character from the popular and newly launched *Mad* magazine, "What, me worry?"

Fortunately for the rest of us, Nils Bohlin (1920–2002)—Volvo engineer and the inventor of the three-point shoulder harness—was worried. Swedes have long been justifiably credited with

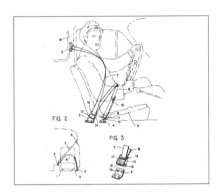

FIG 2

FIG 3

creating some of the safest and most sensible vehicles on the planet, but in a nation of anti-Alfred E. Neuman engineers, Mr. Bohlin stands out. His invention, basically unchanged and used in all new cars today, is credited with saving more lives than any other safety device ever installed in an automobile. Now there is a sensible guy.

Bohlin's seat-belt design first saw production in Volvo's 120-series models, which appeared in 1959—a full 10 years before being adopted by American manufacturers who only got on the bandwagon when the federal government forced them.

A sensible, four-cylinder model also known as the Amazon, these Volvos were known in the United States as the 122. Apart from the shoulder harness, the 122 is not particularly remembered for much, other than outstanding reliability. Many are still on the road today—helped, in part, by a long production run that continued largely

unchanged through the 1968 model year. The 122 was available in two- or four-door sedan models, along with a popular station wagon version. A performance model, the 123 GT, is the most prized by collectors today, but a station wagon with original tires, a plastic-covered driver's seat, and fewer than 100 miles on the odometer was recently sold on eBay for close to $30,000.

That said, the shoulder harness is what really sets this model apart, and which presumably helped keep many of its owners on the road. Most cars did not even have lap belts in 1959, and the government did not mandate their installation until the 1966 model year. Even then, they were required only for front-seat passengers. Front-seat shoulder harnesses were not mandatory in the United States until 1974.

Left: Nils Bohlin filed for a U.S. patent on his three-point safety belt in 1959.

Below: Volvo 122s were reliable cars and can still be seen on the road today.

Chrysler Turbine Car

Of the 55 Turbine Cars that Chrysler built from 1963 to 1964, only a handful exist today. The rest, containing hand built bodies and engines, were crushed.

For years, the Chrysler Corporation had flirted with the idea of building production turbine-powered cars before the eventual introduction of the car most commonly associated with the program, known simply as the Turbine Car. Powered by what was actually Chrysler's fourth-generation turbine engine, the carmaker built 55 identical two-door coupes from 1963 to 1964. Then, they put them for free into the hands of "average" consumers and let them have at it, in order to help determine the viability of bringing a turbine to production—and get some valuable publicity at the same time.

All of the Turbine Cars sported a bronze paint job, a vinyl top covering (as was popular at the time), and leather interiors, as well as power steering, brakes, and windows. Bodies were built by coachbuilder Ghia of Italy, based on a

design inspired by airplanes and reminiscent of period Ford styling motifs (the director of design, Elwood Engel, had previously been at Ford). The headlights, taillights, and other components were actually styled to look like jet turbines.

First announced to the public in 1963, the Turbine Cars became a sensation with both the press and the public at the 1964 New York World's Fair. The cars were then provided to a total of about 200 different families at no charge, with each family taking a three-month stint behind the wheel. Applicants for the program had to be licensed drivers who already owned cars, but that did not stop at least one 12-year-old boy from signing on. Sadly for him, he was denied.

Operating instructions stated that the cars were pretty normal to drive, using a conventional key to start the engine. The situation changed from there. Within a few seconds, the inlet temperature gauge read 1,700° F (926.7° C), and the tachometer stood at 22,000 rpm, meaning that you were good to go. With that kind of temperature and engine speed, one would hope so.

One of the major appeals of the turbine design was fewer moving parts than a conventional piston engine, and, as was hoped anyway, better reliability. Hand-built at Chrysler's Research Center, each car could run on any combination of jet fuel, diesel, kerosene, or even vegetable oil. Consumption of any of the above was high—which was one of the Turbine Car's main problems.

Another was exhaust heat—the turbine radiated so much of it that stories exist of asphalt being burned below the cars while they idled at stoplights. High amounts of oxides of nitrogen were also reported in the exhaust. Yet another problem, and one of the chief complaints of test users, was simply the noise of the thing. The turbine was often compared to the sound of a giant vacuum cleaner, in a

time when most drivers were accustomed to the satisfying thrum of a big V8. There were also complaints about throttle lag—the engine took its time to get going after the accelerator was pressed.

In the end, the Turbine Car never made it past the testing stage. Of the 55 hand-built test cars made, only a few survive today. Most were crushed in compliance with Federal import laws, their hand-built, Italian bodies having been imported for test-use only. Chrysler kept a couple for exhibition, and provided a few more to various museums, after rendering their engines inoperable. At least one, and probably more of those donated cars are rumored to have ended up in the hands of private collectors, and restored so their turbines could spin again.

The cost of restoring these automotive artifacts was presumably significant, but at least the Turbine Car's owners can take comfort in the fact their car will run on just about anything.

Below: All Chrysler turbine engines were hand built at the Chrysler Research Center.

Background: This vintage Chrysler publicity shot shows the Turbine Car's aircraft-inspired design features.

Volkswagen Beetle

It is hard to argue that another car in existence is more recognizable than the Volkswagen Beetle. Even people with no interest in or knowledge of cars can point one out in traffic, and its distinctive shape has inspired all kinds of backseat games for kids, from simply counting them, to the not-so-pleasant "Punch Buggy" jabs often exchanged by siblings upon seeing one.

The recognition is justified. With more than 22 million models sold, the original Beetle is by far the biggest selling single car in history. More people around the world either owned one, were the sons or daughters of parents who bought one, or at least rode in one at some point, than any other car in history. For baby boomers especially, the ubiquitous Bug has been hard to avoid.

First envisioned as the People's

Volkswagen produced the Beetle for more than 50 years, eventually selling over 22 million models.

SPECIFICATIONS

1967 VOLKSWAGEN BEETLE
Top speed: 82 mph (132 km/h)
Engine: Air-cooled, 1.2 liter, four-cylinder
engine rated at 53 hp (39 kw) at
4,200 rpm and 78 lb ft (106 nm) of
torque at 2,600 rpm

Car (in German, *volks wagen*) by Adolf Hitler, the idea behind the Bug was to bring affordable personal transportation to the masses. Designer Ferdinand Porsche (1875–1951) came up with a simple concept that met Hitler's basic requirements: The car must be capable of carrying a family, able to travel at 62 miles (100 km) per hour, return 33 miles per gallon, and cost no more than 990 reichsmark, at a time when

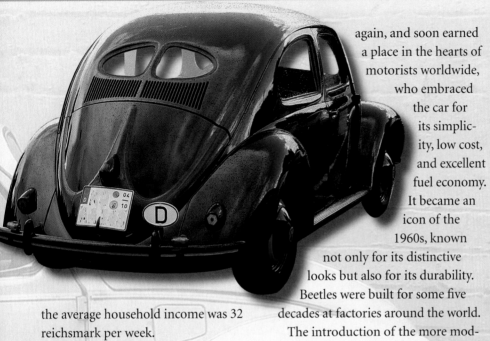

Left: A 1950 Volkswagen Beetle, recognizable by its split rear window and small, rounded taillights.

Background: The profile of the Volkswagen Beetle is probably more widely recognized than any other car design.

again, and soon earned a place in the hearts of motorists worldwide, who embraced the car for its simplicity, low cost, and excellent fuel economy. It became an icon of the 1960s, known not only for its distinctive looks but also for its durability. Beetles were built for some five decades at factories around the world.

the average household income was 32 reichsmark per week.

Early prototypes were tested with various engines, but an air-cooled, flat-four design (so named because the pistons are mounted horizontally) eventually won out, a configuration that the Beetle stayed with until the last one was built in 2003. Never known for neck-snapping acceleration, early Beetles had as little as 22 horsepower. This number climbed ever so slowly throughout its more than half a century on the road.

The outbreak of World War II meant that any production capability to build the People's Car went instead to building variants more useful to the war effort. Once the war was over, however, Beetles started rolling off assembly lines

The introduction of the more modern Rabbit brought an end to American sales of the Beetle sedan in 1978, and after a successful run it became a victim of aging design and more sophisticated needs for safety and emissions equipment. However, production continued in Mexico until 2003, where the simplicity, reliability, and economy of the aging design were still marketable to a less-discriminating audience.

The legend lives on, as Volkswagen reintroduced the New Beetle in 1998. Though water-cooled and front-engined, the reincarnation carries nearly the same shape as the original—and Punch Buggy jabs have been introduced to a whole new generation.

Mini

Sir Alec Issigonis (1906–88) was more than your average visionary. The designer of the original Mini not only brought a sensible, economical, and affordable car to the marketplace at a time when the world was ready for one, he devised a whole new way to package automobiles that is copied by designers around the world to this day, including those at BMW who penned the popular new Mini.

The original of 1959 was a small, front-wheel-drive car with its engine mounted sideways, or transversely. This made for a more compact engine compartment, and more room for passengers. Made by the now-defunct British Motor Corporation, Issigonis's iconic design went on to become the biggest selling car in Europe, and some five-million units were sold around the world before production ended in 2000. An international poll ranked it as one of the most influential cars of all time, second only to the Model T Ford.

In addition to the benefits of front-wheel-drive traction, the Mini's unique design allowed for four adults to ride in a car barely three meters (9.8 ft) long, and made it easy to park and maneuver on city streets. As a bonus, the tiny Mini was a blast to drive, even if it was short on creature comforts. Sir Issigonis was not a fan of such things as radios, let alone the power windows and locks that drivers take for granted today. Issigonis had no interest in coddling drivers, whom he felt should be paying attention to the task at hand.

Something of an eccentric, Sir Alec was once said to have preferred that his passengers sit on nails rather than have comfy seats. At least he practiced what he preached—he never even had a radio in his own car. Mini buyers put up with features like doors opened with a pull cord, sliding plastic windows, and bare steel surfaces in the cabin. What else would you expect from a guy who described market research as "bunk." At least a radio was offered as an option.

Even with its Spartan interior, the Mini became such a hit that the design spawned pickup truck, station wagon, and van variants, and the car even became a favorite on race circuits—

SPECIFICATIONS

1966 AUSTIN MINI COOPER S
Top speed: 100 mph (161 km/h)
Engine: 1.3 liter, four-cylinder engine rated at 78 hp (57.4 kw) at 5,800 rpm and 80 lb ft (108.5 nm) of torque at 3,000 rpm

The interior of a 1959 Morris Mini-Minor, minimal and utilitarian, just as Alec Issigonis wanted it.

something else Alec had little interest in, even though his design won the Monte Carlo rally three times.

Power was modest, with engines ranging in size from the original 34-horsepower, 848 cubic-centimeter (51.75 cu. in.) model to the later, high-performance Cooper S version, with 1275 cc (77.8 cu. in.). However, the Mini's lightness and independent suspension helped give it handling often described as go-cartlike. The diminutive cars developed a worldwide following of fans that continues to this day, and their cultlike status in the 1960s was partly fueled by celebrity owners including members of the Beatles, actors Steve McQueen and Peter Sellers, and even Enzo Ferrari. Minis had a starring role in 1969's *The Italian Job*, a performance that was repeated in the 2003 remake of the film—this time using the new, reincarnated Mini, which has become something of a cult classic itself.

A 1967 Morris Mini-Minor. With front-wheel drive and its engine mounted sideways to maximize passenger room, the layout of the Mini became a small-car blueprint still used by designers today.

SIR ALEC ISSIGONIS

If there is such a thing as a typical car designer, Alec Issigonis was not that type of individual. Most famously remembered for the Mini, Issigonis's designs also included the Morris Minor, parts of various military vehicles during World War II, and a handmade wood and aluminum-bodied racing car he built with a friend early in his career. They used no power tools in its construction, and Alec went on to successfully compete in the car, dubbed the Lightweight Special.

Never interested in cars as a young boy, Issigonis was 12 years old before he even rode in one. A road trip fraught with mechanical difficulties that he took after graduating from engineering school finally led him into an automotive career.

Always a strong-headed, independent thinker, Issigonis single-handedly originated most of the design and specifications of the Morris Minor, which was highly unusual even in the 1940s. Like the more revolutionary Mini that followed, the Minor was a huge success and remained in production from 1948 to 1971.

Chrysler K-Car

SPECIFICATIONS

1981 PLYMOUTH RELIANT/ DODGE ARIES
0–60 mph (0–97 km/h): 13 sec
Engine: 2.2 liter, in-line four-cylinder engine with electric carburetor rated at 84 hp (63 kw) at rpm and 111 lb ft (150 nm) of torque at rpm

In September 1979, the Chrysler Corporation came hat-in-hand to the U.S. government, seeking $1.5 billion in loan guarantees to avoid bankruptcy. Chrysler was reeling from the collapse of its European division and the unfortunate decision to continue making mostly big cars and few economical models, which left it hurting during the second American oil crisis.

The carmaker brought in a charismatic former Ford executive, Lee A. Iacocca (b. 1924), to take the reins of the company. He touted a new direction that stressed restructuring the company and designing a single compact-car platform that would become the cornerstone of its entire product line.

For the company to survive, any vehicle it introduced had to be a resounding hit. Chrysler had to sell their prospective platform, the K, to the government before they sold it to the public. Executives testified before Congress that these inexpensive, front-wheel drive, four-cylinder cars would become the automaker's predominant vehicles and would steer it back to profitability. Congress remained skeptical, but passed the "Chrysler Corporation Loan Guarantee Act" in late 1979. President Jimmy Carter signed it into law early the next year.

Production of the K-Car began in mid-1980 with the 1981 Dodge Aries and Plymouth Reliant. The longer Chrysler LeBaron was introduced the next year and other variations followed, including the luxurious Chrysler New Yorker and sporty Chrysler Laser/ Dodge Daytona.

Despite being mostly basic, unexceptional cars, the K platform proved to be a huge hit with gas price-wary buyers. Iacocca, who was also drafted into service as a corporate pitchman, was so convincing with his television delivery that speculation arose about a presidential run in his future.

The Reliant, Aries, and LeBaron became particularly strong-selling vehicles. Chrysler was able to reduce production costs by using the same parts to build many models, and did not even make component modifications for vehicles as disparate as sport coupes and luxury cars. The K-Car platform even formed the basis for that most ubiquitous of modern

Chrysler products, the first front-wheel drive minivan, which became the standard family hauler for a generation of soccer moms, dads, and players.

By the early 1980s, Chrysler was quickly paying back its loan guarantees. The sale of its defense division to General Dynamics in 1982 put the company even closer to profitability. And in August 1983, Chrysler paid back its government-backed loan guarantees seven years ahead of schedule—with full interest. Chrysler stock, which was selling at around five dollars per share just before the introduction of the K-Car, was now selling at 30 dollars per share.

The humble K-Car had saved the company.

A Chrysler LeBaron sedan, one of the various models that utilized the K-Car platform, which is credited with saving the struggling carmaker from bankruptcy.

CHAPTER 6

MILITARY VEHICLES

THE FIRST KNOWN SELF-PROPELLED military vehicles were a trio of electric autos built by Woods Motor Company in 1899. The U.S. Army requested these vehicles—two light trucks and a scout car—to assist with operations in the Philippines during the Spanish-American War.

Not until 1916, when General John J. Pershing needed a fleet of motorized vehicles to outmaneuver the cavalry of Mexican rebel Francisco "Pancho" Villa, was the military's relationship with the automobile cemented.

Ever since, the military's appetite for innovative vehicles has spurred many great engineering advances, some of which eventually found their way into passenger cars. Many of these developments, such as more efficient engines, heavy-duty differentials, electrical circuit breakers, and sturdier suspensions, may not be particularly exciting stuff, but are significant nonetheless. Others, including four-wheel drive, run-flat tires, tire-pressure monitoring, and flexible-fuel capability were either designed for, or first widely used on, military vehicles.

To anticipate the future of the automobile, one need not look much further than the direction today's military is heading. Technologies such as modular drive-by-wire components, electric propulsion, exportable electric power, and advanced night-vision optics are said to be included on next-generation fighting vehicles. Then after that, they may well be incorporated into the family car.

Left: A U.S. Marine driving through the sand at Iwo Jima during World War II. The versatile, reliable Jeep became a favorite with GIs and served a variety of wartime duties. Inset: Like the Jeep that it replaced in United States military duty, the Humvee has served in a number of combat roles.

Jeep

On the eve of World War II, the United States military needed a rugged, versatile scout car for the impending conflict. Three manufacturers built prototypes to government specifications—Ford, Willys-Overland, and the smaller American Bantam.

Bantam had enlisted the help of automotive designer Karl Probst (1883–1963) and quickly devised a prototype to show the government. Ford and Willys followed with similar prototypes that many believed were copied from Bantam's engineering specifications. Because Bantam was a small car company with limited manufacturing assets, the contract was granted to Willys. Soon after, Ford was also contracted to build their version of the scout car.

The government's four-wheel-drive requirement earned the conceptual vehicle the nickname of "quad." However, by the time Willys began production, the scout cars were already dubbed "Jeeps,"

in likely reference to Eugene the Jeep, a bearlike comic-strip creature that could walk through walls and on ceilings. Many felt that the military's Jeep had similar "go anywhere" potential. Another story holds that the name was based on the Ford version's designation of GP, which indicated that it was a "government" vehicle; other sources claim that GP stood for "general purpose." All in all, there are many apocryphal origins for the vehicle's name. The first-known use of the term "Jeep" in print came from a February 1941 article in the *Washington Daily News*, when it was reported that one scaled the steps of the Capitol Building.

During the war, many credited the vehicle as being pivotal to Allied success. Folksy war correspondent Ernie Pyle, whose articles appeared in more than 200 newspapers across America, was quick to praise the Jeep, which gave it a legendary status back home. Willys-Overland harnessed the phenomenon, and as far back as 1942, began running advertisements touting them as potential civilian vehicles.

SPECIFICATIONS

1941 WILLYS MB JEEP
Top speed: 62 mph (100 km/h)
Engine: In-line four-cylinder engine rated at
60 hp (45 kw) at 3,600 rpm and 105 lb ft
(142 nm) of torque at 2,000 rpm

This is one of the prototypes of the military Jeep, constructed by Bantam in 1940. This model, now in the Smithsonian collection, was the seventh test vehicle built in a series of 62.

Sure enough, with the Jeep's legacy etched into the American lexicon by the war's end, the CJ, which stood for "Civilian Jeep," was introduced. Although only Ford's wartime Jeeps had grilles with metal slats, Willys introduced the seven-slat grille on the CJ, and it has since evolved into one of the vehicle's most noticeable trademarks.

Willys sought and was granted the "Jeep" trademark in 1950. Three years later, Willys was sold to Kaiser Industries, which was bought by American Motors in 1970, which in turn was acquired by Chrysler in 1988, which merged with Daimler-Benz in 1998, only to be recently sold to the private equity firm Cerberus in 2007.

For some 60 years, there was no significant redesign of the Jeep, and structural modifications came at a snail's pace. One Jeep iteration, the CJ-5, actually lasted 30 years, from 1953 to 1983.

By 1987, Jeep had lost its military contract and a revamped civilian-only vehicle was dubbed the Wrangler. That design remained pretty much unchanged for 20 years. By the 21st century, the Wrangler had become a "retro car," much like the New Beetle and the modern Mini, since it looked pretty much the same as the scout car that Ernie Pyle bragged about. The difference was that the Jeep did not just look retro—it truly was an old, outdated design.

Buying the Wrangler was more of a fashion statement, as there were many more competent sport-utility vehicles in the market. There was nothing nostalgic about its outdated engineering. It began to receive poor reviews from automotive and consumer magazines alike. More modern and comfortable Jeep models, like the Grand Cherokee, began to outsell the Wrangler, though it still remained the very essence and image of Jeep.

For the 2007 model year, the Wrangler received its first total overhaul and did not inherit any components from the previous version. The result is a much more refined vehicle that still retains the classic looks and "go anywhere" attributes that made it famous.

The WWII success of the Jeep led to versions for civilian use. Variations of the original CJs, or Civilian Jeeps, are still sold today. This one, a Jeep Wrangler from 1992, uses rectangular headlights, which were popular at the time.

Half-Track

Right: Half-tracks served on missions to unexplored parts of the planet as well as taking part in military duty. This one, a 1934 Citröen P17 series D, was used by Charles Bedeaux to explore northern Alberta, Canada.

The half-track was invented in the 1910s, and many people shared credit for its rudimentary design. Adolphe Kégresse (1879–1943) was perhaps the individual most responsible for its creation, though. Kégresse was commissioned by Russian czar Nicholas II to convert several cars to travel in the snowy and muddy conditions common in Russia. Kégresse mated the rear-drive axle of a conventional vehicle with an arrangement of wheels that drove a reinforced, treaded, flexible belt, which was wrapped around them. The front axle, however, was linked to conventional tires and wheels.

Soon after World War I, Kégresse began working for French automaker Citroën, where he developed similar half-track vehicles that were often used to explore the desert regions of northern Africa.

In the buildup to U.S. involvement in World War II, the American army recognized the need for vehicles that could travel in harsh off-road conditions, yet handle like a typical wheeled vehicle. It purchased several Citroën half-tracks for evaluation. Soon after, it obtained a license to produce them. The army used what it had learned from the Kégresse design and began developing half-tracks with the White Motor Company—which at the time was also developing the M3 Scout Car, a vehicle used early in the war effort that was doomed to obsolescence because of its limited seating and insufficient capabilities when the going got really rough. White used the front body of the M3 and matched it with a different drivetrain and rear chassis to create its version of the half-track. Two basic designs were devised: The smaller M2

Below: The M3 A1 half-track was developed by White Motor Company and used by Allied forces during World War II. It carried up to 10 passengers.

carried a crew of up to seven men and was fitted with a Browning machine gun. The more powerful M3 was faster than the M2, equipped with two machine guns, and carried up to 10 passengers.

The half-tracks underwent numerous updates and were customized for the varied and difficult duties they were tasked to perform. The resulting variations and alphanumeric designations are enough to confuse all but the best parts-counter people, and appear endless, even to half-track aficionados. While some half-tracks were used primarily for armored infantry transport, variations that followed included ordnance and supply carriers, and self-propelled mortar, artillery, and anti-aircraft artillery configurations.

The military's demand for half-tracks was greater than White's production capacity. Not long after White began production, two other companies,

Diamond T Motor Car and Autocar, were also contracted to build half-tracks. Between them, they produced some 43,000 vehicles.

In 1941, International Harvester was commissioned to create its own version of the M2 and M3 half-tracks, called the M9 and M5, respectively. These were sent to Europe to support allies such as Great Britain, France, and the Soviet Union. The M5 and M9, though very similar to the American vehicles, used different engines and drivetrains.

Despite being effective on the battlefield, advances in both wheeled and track vehicles caused the United States to abandon development of half-tracks soon after World War II. However, modified World War II half-tracks remained in commission in both Argentina and Israel at the start of the twenty-first century.

Allied half-tracks and tanks parade along the Champs Elysees after Paris was liberated on August 25, 1944.

The HMMWV or Humvee

In the late 1970s, the Department of Defense realized that it didn't have a versatile vehicle that could cut it on the modern battlefield. The World War II-vintage Jeep and militarized versions of civilian light trucks were not up for the job. Specifications were drawn up for a "High Mobility Multipurpose Wheeled Vehicle" (HMMWV) that could be easily modified to perform varied tasks on the battlefield. In 1981, the Army awarded AM General, a subsidiary of American Motors, the development contract to build testing prototypes, and later gave the company an initial production contract for 55,000 vehicles.

Variations of the original M998 HMMWV design became ambulances, troop carriers, missile carriers, and cargo carriers. Today, there are dozens of specialized military applications for the vehicle. Perhaps because the abbreviation HMMWV was awkward and too hard to pronounce as an acronym even by armed forces standards,

U.S. Marines and their Humvees in Saudi Arabia in 1991, in the early days of the Persian Gulf War, known in the United States as Operation Desert Storm.

SPECIFICATIONS

1995 AM GENERAL M998A2 HMMWV
Top speed: 83 mph (134 km/h)
Engine: 6.5 liter V8 engine rated at 160 hp
(117.8 kw) at 3,400 rpm and 290 lb ft
(393 nm) of torque at 1,700 rpm

it was phonetically shortened to "Humvee" by both the military and the media.

The Humvee had its first taste of fame after being used during the Panamanian uprising in 1989 and in the Gulf War of 1990. Actor turned California governor Arnold Schwarzenegger, impressed by the Humvees he used in one of his movies, ratcheted up the buzz when he announced his intention to purchase one.

Sensing a civilian market for its new four-wheeled star, AM General began to market the Humvee under the brand name "Hummer" in 1991. The vehicle was an instant hit, even with a price tag of more than $60,000. Instead of weapons fittings or other military paraphernalia, the civilian Hummer included creature comforts such as a stereo system and air conditioning. The civilian version also ran on a 12-volt system like other street vehicles; the HMMWV uses a 24-volt system.

"Hummer is a very profitable brand for General Motors, very profitable."

—Bob Lutz, General Motors Vice Chairman

In 1999, AM General sold the Hummer brand to General Motors, but continued to manufacture it as the H1. General Motors designed a somewhat smaller and more practical version for suburbanites with a fondness for camouflaged clothing and the films of Mr. Schwarzenegger. Based on a GM truck platform, AM General was contracted to build the H2. In 2006, GM introduced the H3, based on its small-truck platform, and took on manufacturing duties itself. Not long after the introduction of the H3, GM discontinued civilian sales of the H1, which had dwindled to a few hundred units per year.

Meanwhile, the Humvee began to get poor marks, some of which it perhaps may not have deserved, for its performance in the Iraq War. Created for mobility through varying terrains, the Humvee was not intended for urban combat or as an armored-personnel carrier, but it was thrust into this role for the Iraq War. Also, without armor, as many of them were deployed, the Humvee has proved to be quite vulnerable to weapons' fire, land mines, and improvised explosive devices created by Iraqi insurgents. The Humvees that were armored, either with military-supplied kits or with armor improvised by troops—known as "hillbilly armor"—proved to be slow, unwieldy, and very inefficient.

In late 2006, the Department of Defense began to seek a replacement for the Humvee as its primary multi-purpose vehicle. AM General was not selected as a candidate for the creation of a prototype.

The Hummer H2 helped General Motors cash in on the popularity that Humvees had developed in a nation watching 24-hour war coverage and already addicted to SUVs.

Bulletproof Vehicles

Al Capone saw the value in a personal armored vehicle long before it became fashionable. His 1928 Cadillac, seen here, was steel plated, and contained a powerful six-cylinder engine.

Armored vehicles are more widely used today than ever before by the military, government officials, business tycoons, and even private individuals (some probably have good reasons not to discuss their need for one). Bulletproof vehicles are hardly a new idea. Trucks reinforced with steel were used for military duty as far back as the Spanish-American War, and crime boss Al Capone famously had his 1928 Cadillac steel-plated to protect him from the guns of rival gangsters.

Armored vehicles were not mass produced for civilians until the early 1980s, when the Stutz Motor Car Company modified a Chevrolet Suburban SUV, dubbed it the Defender, and started making sales, primarily to Middle Eastern heads of state. The Defender—and a four-door convertible version, the Bear—gained popularity partly because they did not draw much unwanted attention, yet were able to protect the occupants from weapons fire and explosives. An important design feature of modern armored vehicles is to look as much like a normal car or truck as possible, so would-be bad guys do not think anybody important is inside.

Today's armored civilian vehicles are not only popular with diplomats, but also with executives, military contractors, and relief workers employed in unstable areas such as war zones. In parts of the world known for less-than-stable governments, and particularly in areas notable for a robust drug trade, a bulletproof ride is often a sought-after item by any family who can afford one.

Chevy Suburbans remain a popular choice with individuals who fear that there is somebody gunning for them. However, a wide variety of other models, from basic Volkswagen Golfs to Mercedes-Benz M-Class SUVs, are converted by companies who specialize in transforming them into rolling safety pods with bulletproof glass, ballistic-steel plating, and run-flat tires that enable the driver to keep moving even after a tire is punctured by a sniper. It all depends on the budget and needs of the customer.

More exotic materials are used in addition to steel, such as strong but lightweight Kevlar, long used by police departments for bulletproof vests. Kevlar saves weight over metal, and as a woven material, it can be easily shaped to fit around wheel wells and in curved door panels before hardening resins are added to give it rigidity.

Companies specializing in the manufacture of armored vehicles for either military or civilian use are justifiably not very forthcoming about the details of their designs, or who is buying them. They need to keep a low profile, too. But other popular features include sirens, automatic fire extinguishers, sealed air supplies to combat gas attacks, and machine guns hidden beneath the sheet metal. Armored vehicles often also have engines modified with increased horsepower and improved brakes to offset their increased weight.

Most cars and SUVs are modified in the aftermarket, but manufacturers including BMW and Audi produce armored versions of their larger sedans. A typical armored conversion of a car or SUV can cost as much as $100,000.

While not exactly a low-profile vehicle, the Chevrolet Suburban–based Bear proved popular in the Middle East. With the stock roof removed however, one can only assume that occupants knew when to duck.

CHAPTER 7

GREEN CARS

AS GAS PRICES RISE AND CONCERN for the environment grows, car manufacturers and entrepreneurs alike continue to work to develop alternatives to the gasoline-fueled car.

These alternatives are often referred to as green cars. Generally speaking, a green car uses an alternative fuel for some or all of its power. These fuels can include electricity, ethanol, biodiesel, hydrogen, natural gas, steam, solar, wood, or a combination of these. Some green cars even run on used vegetable oil available from a local fast-food restaurant or diner.

Drivers today can choose from ever-increasing options depending on their financial resources, personal preferences, and how much they are willing to roll up their sleeves and get involved in obtaining and refining the fuel themselves.

Current interest in green cars is also an example of history repeating itself. Electric cars have been around for more than 100 years, and inventors have been experimenting with alternative fuels ever since the invention of the automobile. As humanity's appetite for both energy and personal mobility continues, expect development of these alternatives—as well as new technologies— to continue faster than ever.

No longer strictly minimal transportation, today's green cars include electrics capable of 100 miles (161 km) per hour, and hybrids that return both excellent fuel economy and rock-solid reliability. Here is a look at a few of them.

Honda has been developing the FCX, its hydrogen fuel-cell vehicle, since the 1990s. The first model was produced in 1999, and a new sedan version is slated to come out in 2008. Hydrogen fuel cells generate power by mixing hydrogen with oxygen to create electricity.

Early Electric Cars

Though electric cars may seem like a futuristic concept, they were actually among the earliest automobiles. In the early 20th century, they rivaled gasoline-powered cars in popularity.

The earliest-known electric car was built by William Morrison and made its debut in Des Moines, Iowa, in 1890. "The Electric Buggy," as Morrison dubbed it, was a seven-passenger vehicle that tickled the fancy of the public, who read about it in newspapers and magazines such as *Scientific American.* However, Morrison had little interest in manufacturing automobiles. He soon sold his buggy and later denounced horseless carriages, saying, "I wouldn't pay ten cents for an automobile for my own use."

Morrison's feelings notwithstanding, electric cars, also called "juicers" by aficionados, met with commercial success soon after. In 1897, the Electric Carriage & Wagon Company was commissioned to build a fleet of electric taxis for New York City. Other companies followed soon after, including Rauch & Lang, Baker Electric, and Detroit Electric.

In the early 20th century, many buyers found clean and silent electric cars to be preferable to their dirty and noisy internal-combustion counterparts. Electrics were also free from the vibrations that plagued early gasoline-powered cars, and perhaps most importantly, they had no need for a difficult and dangerous hand-crank starter.

A 1914 Rauch and Lang electric automobile. With much quieter operation and higher prices than gas-powered cars of their time, early electrics were a favorite with wealthy urbanites. One such owner—Marie D. Gorgas, the wife of the 22nd Surgeon General of the U.S. Army, William C. Gorgas—donated this one to the Smithsonian.

Because electric cars were so civilized by comparison, wealthy women often purchased them as city cars. Doctors were also fond of electrics, and legend has it that when making house calls, some would take along an X-ray machine and hook it up to the car's battery when visiting patients without electricity in their homes.

Without mechanical components like large tombstone-like radiators, they were among the first vehicles to incorporate a sweeping design and their interiors were considered quite opulent. The Rauch & Lang electric car, which sold for $3,800 in 1912, was considered to be the pinnacle of luxurious motoring. By 1914, some 4,600 electric cars were sold in the United States, comprising a significant portion of the automotive market.

However, the shortcomings of electric cars soon became evident. An infrastructure with refilling stations and paved roads between cities was being built and electric-car owners could not take advantage of it. Electric cars had a limited range of only about 50 miles (80 km) and required an overnight recharging with special equipment. Later, internal-combustion vehicles became more powerful and attained speeds well beyond the slow 20 miles (32.2 km) per hour that electric cars could reach.

By 1920, gasoline cars had realized many improvements; they were becoming quieter and cleaner, but best of all, the arduous hand-crank starter had given away to the easy-to-use electric starter. That year, Rauch & Lang, the last of the electric-car makers, stopped producing electric cars for consumers. They stuck around for a few more years producing electric taxis before finally closing up shop.

Above: This Riker electric automobile, built around 1900, looked like it could be pulled by a horse. Perhaps this made it a more comfortable purchase for early motorists. It is now in the collection of the Smithsonian Institution.

Below: Now part of the Smithsonian collection, a Dr. J.O. Skinner owned this 1904 Columbia electric car from 1906 to 1931. He presumably used it to make faster house calls than were possible by horse and buggy.

Vegetable Oil–Powered Cars

One of the more interesting alternative fuels available for motorists trying not to fatten the wallets of oil executives is the vegetable oil–powered car, sometimes known as a greasecar. Also known as SVOs, for straight-vegetable-oil-compatible, these vehicles can be powered by either new vegetable oil, or, for more ambitious greasers (as some refer to themselves), used oil from restaurant deep fryers.

There is a problem though: Owners have said that the exhaust fumes, which reportedly smell like deep-fried food, can lead drivers to crave onion rings and egg rolls. The bigwigs' wallets may become thinner, but greasecar owners run the risk of putting on a few pounds.

Proponents of the fuel say that virtually any diesel-powered car can be converted to run on veggie oil, with no ill effects. Several companies offer conversion kits, and their Web sites feature testimonials from happy greasecar

users with stories of successful, albeit artery-endangering motoring.

The best part is that the fuel can be had for free if you find a cooperative restaurateur. Every year, about 100-million gallons of waste vegetable oil is generated in the United States, and the stuff has to go someplace. The greaser grapevine says that large chains are usually out as a fuel source, due to a combination of oil additives and franchise-related red tape. Independent restaurants, which often have to pay to have waste oil removed, are said to be generally willing to negotiate with motorists who wish to cart it away.

Like fans of some other alternative fuels, SVO devotees have to be prepared to work a little harder for a fill-up than credit card–toting folks, even after they have found a fuel source. The oil must be filtered before use, a multi-stage process that involves more than just putting it through a hankie to trap stray french fries. Once the filtering is done, toting and storing bulky containers is the next step of the program, as is, of course, transferring the fuel to their car at the risk of a bath best described as unpleasant. Once all that is done, greasecars must still be run on conventional diesel when first started, and again before they are shut off to prevent veggie oil—which will congeal at temperatures of 90° F (32° C), and will gum up fuel lines, filters, and injectors if not preheated—from clogging the fuel system. That means retaining the factory diesel fuel tank and installing a second one.

Conversion kits can cost $1,000 or more, and can be more difficult to install than most shade-tree mechanics might be up for. Buyers can opt to pay to have the system installed, which conversion-kit makers can help with. Also, if the business of filtering old fish sticks out of one's fuel is too nasty to consider, the option exists of buying vats of fresh oil at a big-box discounter.

Still, as gas prices continue to rise, the prospect of free fuel only grows in its appeal. And getting rid of waste oil that literally might end up going down the drain is a beautiful concept. The fact that greasecars smell a whole lot better than other diesels is just a bonus.

A happy customer, ready to fuel up. Of all the alternative fuels currently available, vegetable oil is one of the most cost-effective, often available for free.

WILLIE NELSON'S BIODIESEL TOUR BUS

Country music legend Willie Nelson's relationship with biodiesel is not unlike the one a razor magnate once had for his company's product (as was famously touted on ads at the time): He liked it so much, he bought the company.

Clearly, Willie's taste is not for razor technology, but for alternative fuels. He and his wife were so impressed by biodiesel when they first came across it in Hawaii that he converted his tour buses to run on it. The Nelsons have since become investors in biodiesel production plants, and sell it at Carl Cornelius's truck stop in Carl's Corner, Texas, where they pump about 80,000 gallons (302,833 l) of biodiesel blends a day.

Biodiesel is made from vegetable oil, animal fat, soybeans, and other organic compounds and can be blended with conventional diesel fuel.

Willie has become one of the most prominent advocates for the industry, and it is said he even convinced other artists, including Merle Haggard and Asleep at the Wheel, to convert their own tour buses to biodiesel.

General Motors EV1

In 1990, General Motors unveiled a concept vehicle called the Impact at the Los Angeles International Auto Show. An electric car, it became a resounding hit with Californians, who know a thing or two about living with smog. Some credit the Impact as being the driving force behind that state's Zero Emissions Vehicle Mandate, which was passed later that year and required that 2 percent of cars sold there meet the state's zero-emissions standards by 1998.

While other manufacturers started drawing up production plans or modifying existing vehicles to meet this goal, GM developed a purpose-built electric vehicle called the EV1—the only car ever to wear a General Motors nameplate rather than the marque of one of its divisions.

Between 1996 and 1999, GM built 1,117 EV1s and leased them to eager

Inside, the EV1 looked much like other cars of its time, though it sounded much quieter.

Californians and Arizonans. The carmaker heavily subsidized the three-year leases, and there was no option to buy out the lease once it was done. At the end of the term, the lessees had to return the car—a requirement that proved none-too-popular with many of them.

The EV1 could accelerate from zero-to-sixty miles (96.5 km) per hour in less than nine seconds and had a top speed of 80 miles (128.75 km) per hour. Early models were powered by lead-acid batteries, which were later replaced by nickel-metal-hydride batteries that extended the vehicle's range from 75 miles (120.70 km) to 150 miles (241.40 km). The EV1 came with a specialized home charging system, which allowed for relatively quick recharges. Some vehicles also came with a charger that worked with a standard household electrical outlet, but charging times were considerably longer.

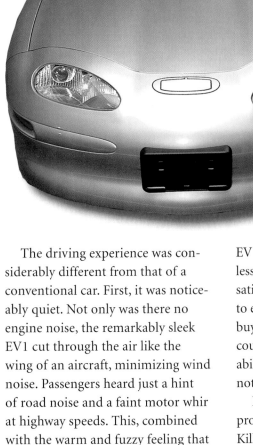

GM killed the EV1 program in 2004, declaring that the car could never be profitable. Critics charged that General Motors never gave the program a chance and anticipated, even orchestrated, its failure. GM maintained that if they could have made the EV1 profitable, they would have. Some lessees were quite vocal in their dissatisfaction about GM's unwillingness to extend their leases or allow them to buy the car. GM stood fast, saying they could not guarantee the safety or reliability of the EV1 over time and would not sell the vehicles.

In 2006, filmmaker Chris Paine produced a documentary called, "Who Killed the Electric Car?" chronicling the demise of California's Zero Emissions Vehicles, particularly the EV1.

The company has since begun development on a new electric/ hybrid platform called E-Flex.

The smooth nose of the EV1 helped maximize its efficiency. It was touted as having "the most aero-dynamic body shape of any production car, ever."

The driving experience was considerably different from that of a conventional car. First, it was noticeably quiet. Not only was there no engine noise, the remarkably sleek EV1 cut through the air like the wing of an aircraft, minimizing wind noise. Passengers heard just a hint of road noise and a faint motor whir at highway speeds. This, combined with the warm and fuzzy feeling that ecologically minded EV1 motorists got from doing their part to save the planet, made the popularity of the car understandable among those who leased them.

Honda Civic GX

Natural gas–powered vehicles have been popular for years with fleet users such as municipalities and utilities, who normally have centralized storage and fueling stations for their vehicles—a key asset when you burn a fuel with little or no availability at public stations. Ford, General Motors, and Chrysler have all offered fleet vehicles powered by the clean burning fuel, especially during the 1980s and 1990s.

Compressed natural gas (CNG) is much cleaner-burning than gasoline. According to the Environmental Protection Agency, CNG can reduce carbon-monoxide emissions by 90 to 97 percent and nitrogen-oxide emissions by 35 to 60 percent when compared with gasoline. CNG also produces fewer carcinogenic pollutants.

Natural gas vehicles have other advantages. Because the fuel does not leave hydrocarbon deposits on engine parts, some say these types require less maintenance. Oil changes are typically required at about 10,000 miles (16,093 km), and tune-ups are not required until past 100,000 miles (160,934 km). Engine parts such as valves, cylinders, and piston rings are also said to undergo much less wear than those of conventional cars.

Proponents say that the fuel is also much less of a fire hazard than gasoline. Instead of pooling around a vehicle in the event of an accident, natural gas disperses into the air, reducing risk of a fire. If all that is not enough to make you want to trot out and buy a car powered by the fuel, experts say the United States has plenty of natural gas reserves, which, unlike gasoline, reduces the need to rely on foreign sources. As a bonus, the fuel is usually less expensive than gasoline.

However, like many other alternative-fuel vehicles, cars powered by natural gas have suffered from a scarcity of fueling stations. There just are not that many open to the public, and the fuel is not available at all in some states. Reduced maintenance costs where it is available help explain why localized fleet users are some of the most devoted users of CNG.

Fueling up a natural gas–powered Civic. A scarcity of fueling stations is one of the obstacles faced by GX owners.

Honda introduced its own CNG car in 1998. The first Civic GX used a modified 1.6-liter internal combustion engine like that in other Civics. As part of a testing program, several examples of the GX were leased to the city of Los Angeles, where they performed various municipal duties. Driving the original GX was very similar to driving the gasoline-powered version and featured similar performance. However, it only had a range of about 220 miles (354 km), while its gasoline counterparts could travel up to 350 miles (563 km) without refueling.

In 2005, Honda began offering the GX to California consumers. By this time, some 130 CNG fueling stations were in place in the state, which made living with such a vehicle possible in some areas. And while the 2005 GX cost about 25 percent more than a gasoline-powered Civic, fuel savings in the neighborhood of 15 percent helped ease the pain.

In 2006, Honda started selling the updated GX in New York State, which had about fifty CNG fueling stations statewide at the time. The 2006 model also boasted a range of up to 300 miles (483 km) before refueling.

That same year, Honda introduced a device called Phill, a home fueling station for its natural gas–powered Civic, which can charge an empty tank in about 16 hours. Phill, which is about the size of a golf bag, can easily be installed into the garage of a home that has natural-gas service. With a built-in methane detector, Phill monitors for possible, but unlikely, leaks and shuts down if necessary. Phill's manufacturer, the Canadian-based Fuelmaker, says that Phill is as safe as a gas-powered clothes dryer.

Honda has been quietly selling Civic GX sedans to fleet buyers since 1998. The clean-burning cars are now available to consumers in California and New York State.

Toyota Prius

The opening salvo in the current green-car revolution came when Toyota introduced the first-generation Prius to America in 2000. An instant media sensation, the gasoline/electric hybrid vehicle was embraced by environmental types, and soon became the chariot of choice in the limousine lines of Hollywood award ceremonies. To cement the Prius's place in the American lexicon, it became a frequent target of talk radio host Rush Limbaugh, who dismissed the technology behind it and vowed he "wouldn't be caught dead in one."

Despite the hype, the first Prius was indeed a groundbreaking vehicle. Introduced in Japan three years before its American debut, it could run only on batteries, on its gasoline engine, or on a combination of both. Its large nickel-metal-hydride batteries were charged alternately by energy produced by the running engine or by energy reclaimed during braking. When starting and at low speeds, the first Prius, like the second-generation model sold today, was powered only by the quiet electric motor. Upon acceleration, the car's engine would automatically start and provide slightly more zip than most conventional economy cars.

The Prius got 55 miles per gallon (23.35 km/l) in combined city/highway driving according to the EPA, although

tests by outside agencies and publications put mileage at about 10 miles per gallon (4.25 km/l) less. Because of the combination of its small, efficient engine and its use of battery power, the Prius's exhaust contained nearly 90 percent fewer smog-forming emissions than a car powered only by gasoline.

A 2004 redesign bumped a new and larger Prius into midsized-sedan territory. The new Prius used more advanced batteries, got better gas mileage, and could run on the batteries alone in more situations. Critics were quick to point out that fuel savings did not equate to financial savings for the consumer. The Prius's price was some $6,000 to 9,000 more than other sedans in its class, and cost studies showed that it would take several years of driving a Prius to make up its additional cost before the gas savings made it a good deal for the long term.

Under the hood of the Prius a conventional gasoline engine shares space with an electric motor.

Still, the Prius has inspired a cult-like devotion. Its owner-satisfaction rates, according to *Consumer Reports* magazine surveys, have remained consistently higher than any other vehicle on the road for years. The pleasure of owning a Prius, it seems, is not in money saved at the pump, but in the good feeling that owners draw from believing that they are helping to save the Earth.

Some owners still find the fuel economy to be not quite good enough. By 2005, aftermarket retrofit kits were being sold that allowed the Prius to run greater distances on battery power alone and recharge from a standard electrical outlet. Makers claim that these plug-in Priuses can attain the equivalent of 180 miles per gallon (76.43 km/l). However, installing this modification voids the car's warranty. Toyota at first seemed less than pleased that owners were tinkering with their high-tech cars, but the company later announced it would offer its own plug-in feature as an option on future versions of the Prius.

With the Prius, Toyota proved that a gasoline-electric hybrid powerplant could be not only economical, but reliable as well.

Tesla Roadster

Background: A sight that Tesla hopes many highway drivers will be treated to in the near future: the taillights of a Tesla roadster. The Tesla contains no exhaust pipes, because it releases zero emissions.

There has been a widespread assumption that electric cars, if ever produced in large numbers, would not be vehicles to which anybody might become emotionally attached. With designs that have generally been limited to unlovable, anemic subcompacts, it has been a given that consumers would make extreme compromises in space, amenities, and performance in order to have clean, cheap, quiet, and politically-correct motoring.

The General Motors EV1 was the first modern electric car to prove those assumptions wrong, but such beliefs were truly shattered in late 2006, when startup car company Tesla Motors invited 350 guests, including California governor Arnold Schwarzenegger and actor/environmental activist Ed Begley Jr., to the unveiling of their first vehicle, called simply the Roadster. Anything but dull, Tesla's first effort is a supercar, with performance rivaling models like the Dodge Viper, Chevrolet Corvette, and Porsche 911. Tesla claims a zero-to-60 (0–96.5 km) time of 3.9 seconds and a top speed of 130 miles (209.21 km) per hour, and all this with a 250-mile (402.34 km) range—considerably longer than some other electrics.

The performance numbers are astonishing in themselves, but what is more incredible is that the Roadster can do this on only electricity supplied by

lithium ion batteries. Of course, being a supercar, the Roadster has a suitable price tag: the 2008 model sells for $92,000. As of March 2007, orders have been taken for more than 350 of them.

The Roadster owes a lot of its design to British sportscar maker Lotus, known for making cars both light in weight and boasting outstanding handling. The Roadster's chassis comes from the Lotus Elise, along with some dashboard components, windshield, tires, and suspension bits. Tesla's two-seater is then reskinned with its own unique carbon-fiber body.

In addition to Lotus, Tesla Motors teamed with AC Propulsion, a company that converts gas-powered vehicles, like the Scion xB, to electrical drive. The Roadster has a two-speed transmission mated to an electric motor that delivers 248 horsepower and revs up to 13,500 rpm. Tesla calculates fuel economy based on how much power the plug-in car takes from the electrical grid and

claims that it achieves the equivalent mileage of a 135 mpg (57.32 km/l) gasoline-powered automobile.

Tesla also plans to offer a solar-cell recharging system to buyers of the Roadster that will supplement energy used by the home-base charger and allow for 50 miles (80.5 km) of vehicle range per day without using the power grid.

Though it carries a price tag equivalent to a condominium today, future Teslas might be more affordable. The Silicon Valley-based startup claims that guilt-free, spirited motoring will be more accessible to consumers down the road. A sporty luxury sedan with the codename "White Star" is under development for 2010, and the company estimates it will cost between $50,000 and $70,000. A third model, rumored to be even more reasonably priced, is also said to be in the works.

Tesla took electric cars from geekdom to cooldom with their Lotus-based roadster, capable of accelerating from 0–60 mph (0–97 km/h) in 3.9 seconds. The price? $92,000.

WOOD FIRED CARS

When it comes to handing out scores for creative ways to get from point A to point B, some of the highest marks must go to alternative fuel users who operate their vehicles on solid fuel. Solid fuel can consist of many things, including coal, wood, dried sugarcane, old tires, and even cow dung.

Aside from being able to merrily motor along by burning most anything in reach, the other benefit is that unlike those drivers of cars powered by used vegetable oil who report having cravings for french fries, it is unlikely that these motorists are inspired to eat by their cars' emissions.

Some experienced wood burners suggest hauling the wood supply and burner on a trailer in order to minimize the risk of igniting the passenger vehicle and also gaining distance from any insects in the fuel supply.

That sounds like solid advice.

Honda FCX

Concerns about exhaust emissions, global warming, fuel prices, and energy independence have made alternative-fuel vehicles a pressing concern for automakers in the 21st century.

Proposed solutions have included gasoline-electric hybrid technologies, natural gas, biodiesel, and ethanol fuel mixes. However, the Holy Grail of alternative energy for automobiles is hydrogen fuel-cell technology.

Hydrogen fuel cells generate electrical power when hydrogen flows through the cell, where it reacts with oxygen to create electricity and just one byproduct, water vapor. Because there are no toxins or pollutants in the exhaust, vehicles powered by hydrogen fuel cells are considered Zero-Emissions Vehicles.

Honda introduced its first hydrogen-powered vehicle, the FCX, in 1999. Since then, development has continued and the carmaker says it will offer a production version by 2008.

SPECIFICATIONS

HONDA FCX
Top speed: 99 mph (160 km/h)
Range: 354 m (570 km) per charge
Engine: One front-wheel coaxial electric motor rated at 127 hp (95 kw) and 189 lb ft (256 nm) of torque; two rear-wheel electric motors rated at 34 hp (25 kw) each

Honda, more than any other automaker, has championed fuel-cell technology. Honda built their first fuel-cell vehicle, the FCX, in 1999. The FCX had high-pressure hydrogen storage, an array of fuel cells, and a capacitor that stored reserve electricity. This system was coupled with an electric motor that drove the front wheels. It produced eighty horsepower and had a range of 170 miles (274 km).

In 2005, Honda updated the FCX. The small four-passenger hatchback got a boost to 107 horsepower, with 200 pounds-feet (271 nm) of torque, and had an approximate range of 190 miles (306 km). Capable of a zero-to-60 miles (96.5 km) per hour sprint in a respectable 11 seconds, performance was similar to other subcompacts.

The mileage of fuel cell vehicles is measured in miles per kilogram (mpkg) of hydrogen—a measurement that closely correlates to one mile per gallon (0.42 km/l) of gasoline. The 2005 FCX earned an overall 57 mpkg EPA fuel-efficiency rating.

Honda took an unusual tack in the development of the FCX. Instead of developing the car at a test track or under laboratory settings, they produced a small number of FCXs and leased them to a few select customers.

In 2002, the automaker leased five FCXs to the city of Los Angeles. They later leased one to a family in Japan and another to a family in Redondo Beach, California, making the FCX the world's first production fuel-cell vehicle—if only just barely.

Honda introduced a four-door version of the FCX at the 2006 North American International Auto Show, equipped with electric all-wheel drive and a more spacious interior. Slated for production in 2008, Honda says it will produce 129 horsepower and be even more efficient than previous versions of the FCX.

There are major obstacles to overcome before hydrogen fuel-cell cars will be popping up on dealership lots, though. The biggest of which is the decades it might take to build a comprehensive refueling infrastructure for hydrogen-powered vehicles. Honda hopes to solve this problem by developing a Home Energy Station for the FCX. The station will convert natural gas into electricity, heat, and hydrogen, allowing consumers to refuel a fuel-cell vehicle at home and making the FCX a viable automotive option before a reliable infrastructure is in place. In addition to fueling up the car, Honda says that the energy station will also provide home heating and electricity at a significantly lower cost than utility companies.

Welcome to the future. Maybe.

The Honda FC fuel-cell stack, where hydrogen and oxygen mix to produce electricity and wastewater.

Beneath the FCX's futuristic exterior lies an equally futuristic interior.

CHAPTER 8

LEMONS AND CRITICAL FLOPS

THERE ARE CERTAIN CARS, it seems, for which everyone has a soft spot in their hearts. Some are timeless classics that generations of enthusiasts have aspired to own. Others are favorite models that evoke fond memories in those who owned one, whose parents had one, or who knew somebody with one.

Then there are the cars occupying the other end of the emotional spectrum. Cars that, along with their owners, have been the subject of ridicule—sometimes from the day one first appeared in a showroom. Some of these cars were criticized for their styling, but the worst cars actually had serious reliability or safety issues.

In some cases, manufacturers strained to improve these panned or malfunctioning models, occasionally turning them into pretty good cars by the time their production ended—even if it was too late. More often, carmakers just gave up, slashing development and marketing budgets and allowing sales to slow to a trickle before finally pulling the plug. The unfortunate result has been a few more ugly cars on the road at best and some with deadly safety defects at worst.

However, the critics rarely have the last word—most of these critical flops have attracted groups of fans who see beyond their faults and take pride and pleasure in ownership. An abundance of clubs and Web sites are devoted to keeping them on the road, offering tips on maintenance, finding parts, and hosting social events. Photographs of owners posing with beautifully maintained examples are easy to find online.

The Edsel's nose was nothing if not distinctive. But it became the butt of unflattering jokes shortly after the car's 1958 introduction, and probably did little to boost sales.

Edsel

Ah, pity the Edsel. The Rodney Dangerfield of automobiles, if indeed there was one—this is the car that gets no respect. It could have been worse, though. When the Ford Motor Company was trying to coin a name for its new mid-priced car in 1955, it reportedly turned to poet Marianne Moore for ideas. Ms. Moore came up with a few unique suggestions, including Utopian Turtletop and Pastelogram. In the end, the name chosen was that of Henry Ford's son.

Launched with a great deal of fanfare for the 1958 model year, the idea behind the Edsel was to offer Ford buyers a brand to step up to, without making the financial leap to a Mercury or Lincoln. General Motors offered buyers five separate car lines and price ranges at the time, while Ford only had three. The Edsel was offered in four models—the Ranger, the Pacer, the Corsair, and the Citation—and the lofty first-year sales goals were for 200,000 units. However, only 61,000 were sold, with the situation worsening in the next few years.

Originally touted as a whole new kind of car, a marketing ploy recycled by GM for its Saturn division a generation later, the Edsel actually shared most of its components with existing Ford and Mercury models. It did have a few

Edsels were offered as sedans, station wagons, and convertibles like the one shown here. The rare ragtops are the models most valued by collectors today.

"They'll know you've arrived when you drive up in an Edsel."

—FROM A VINTAGE ADVERTISEMENT FOR THE 1958 EDSEL

gimmicks to set it apart, including an automatic transmission controlled by buttons on the steering wheel hub. The system was problematic, though, and added to the Edsel's quickly growing reputation for quality issues.

The styling—particularly the Edsel's snout—is what most potential buyers found off-putting. Described as resembling a Mercury pushing a toilet bowl, the most distinctive styling feature of the Edsel was its elongated, vertical grille.

In hindsight perhaps the Edsel can be seen as no more or less ugly than other cars of the 1950s, but at the time people were not buying it. Literally. Sales dropped to about 45,000 units for the 1959 model year, and the lineup was pared back to just two models.

By the time the 1960 models were introduced, the trademark grille and other styling idiosyncrasies were gone, and Edsels looked pretty much like Fords with different trim. The Edsel had flopped, and the plug was mercifully pulled with only 2,800 examples produced in its final year. Values of used Edsels dropped by as much as $400 overnight after the announcement that the car

had been discontinued—a significant loss at a time when most new models sold for $3,000 or less.

Whether it was the styling, the marketing, the timing, reliability issues as cited by *Consumer Reports*, or, most likely, some combination of the above, the Edsel was history. However, Rangers, Corsairs, and other models live on in the hearts and minds of fans and collectors worldwide.

Maybe they should have gone with Utopian Turtletop.

The last Edsel rolls off the assembly line on November 20, 1959, to little fanfare.

SPECIFICATIONS

1958 EDSEL

Top speed: 105 mph (169 km/h)
0–60 mph (0–97 km/h): 9.7 sec
Engine: 6.7-liter, V8 engine rated at 345 hp (257 kw) at 4,600 rpm, and 475 lb ft (643 nm) of torque at 2,600 rpm

Chevrolet Corvair

The growing popularity of small, fuel-efficient imported cars like the Volkswagen Beetle, combined with a gasoline-happy nation developing an appetite for more than one car per household, led Detroit automakers to introduce smaller models in the early 1960s. It was a savvy move: sales of the smaller models were brisk even as the traditional bread-and-butter sedans continued to grow ever-larger.

While models like the Ford Falcon and Plymouth Valiant were basically shrunken versions of standard domestic offerings, Chevrolet took a more radical approach with the Corvair. With a rear-mounted, air-cooled engine using horizontally mounted cylinders—similar to the Beetle—the Corvair was unlike anything else made in the Motor City.

Chevrolet completely redesigned the Corvair for 1965, keeping the rear-engine layout, but adding a stylish new body and reworked suspension to address rollover concerns. It was already too late however—the perceived failings of earlier models had doomed the car.

Introduced for the 1960 model year, the Corvair was lauded with Car of the Year honors from *Motor Trend* magazine. Despite, or perhaps because of its uniqueness, the Corvair was a success at dealerships, with sales exceeding 200,000 units for a number of years. The line grew to include two- and four-door sedans, turbocharged performance models, convertibles, a van variant, and even a pickup truck with a side-mounted ramp door.

However, the Corvair began a long, slow death with the publication of *Unsafe at Any Speed,* by Ralph Nader, in 1965. While the book was critical of the automotive industry as a whole and devoted only one chapter to the Corvair, it is most often remembered for its definitive condemnation of Chevy's unusual car.

What earned the Corvair a spot in the book was what is called a "swing-arm" rear suspension, which basically puts each wheel at the

"The auto companies had a responsibility to build a crash-worthy car, and the driver had a responsibility to drive safely."

—RALPH NADER

In addition to its unusual rear-mounted engine design, the Corvair was one of the earliest domestic models offered with a turbocharger for more power.

end of an arm hinged in the center of the car. Not an unusual design, swing arms were used at the time by both Volkswagen and Porsche, among others. However, early Corvairs were required to have an unusually low front tire pressure—just 16 pounds per square inch (1.13 kg/cm) cold—to allow for safe handling and compensate for the rearward weight bias of the engine. If the tires were filled to a higher pressure, or if for any reason the front and rear differential became unbalanced, the car could pivot over on the swing axle while cornering and roll over.

A 1964 model-year update mitigated much of the problem, and a total Corvair redesign for 1965 included a four-wheel, independent suspension, advanced for the time and especially unusual in this price range. Borrowing components from the Chevrolet Corvette, the second-generation Corvair suspension helped make it one of the best-handling cars of the time—but it was too late and not just because of Nader.

The Ford Mustang was capturing record sales of buyers looking for a sporty ride, and Chevrolet's Camaro arrived in 1967. Compact buyers could opt for the Chevy Nova, which was enjoying brisk sales without the stigma of the Corvair. Sales went into a slide that would continue until the plug was pulled in 1969, by which time only a few models were offered and both advertising and further development were virtually nil.

In 1971, a National Highway and Traffic Administration study concluded the early Corvair was no more or less dangerous than comparable models of the time.

WHO'S AFRAID OF NADER?

Like many cars scorned by either the critics or the motoring public, Corvairs enjoy a cult following. The Corvair Society of America, or CORSA, takes its name from a high-performance model of the rear-engined car and boasts more than five thousand members worldwide.

Corvairs also have a long and checkered history in road racing. In 1966, Corvette racer Don Yenko created the "Yenko Stinger" for Sports Car Club of America (SCCA)–sanctioned racing by adding horsepower, making suspension upgrades, and removing the backseat to make a Corvair a proper sports car in the eyes of the SCCA. A fast guy on or off the track, in just one month Yenko built the 100 examples required by the SCCA to make the car competition legal.

However, the most adventurous of Corvair fans must be the pilots who build airplanes using their lightweight engines, which they have been doing since the 1960s.

GM Oldsmobile Diesel

In the late 19th century, Rudolf Diesel patented a new type of internal combustion engine. Though diesel-powered cars have been popular in Europe and other parts of the world for decades, they have had limited success in the United States, where gasoline has always been much more affordable than in Europe. In addition, American automotive manufacturers and most car buyers stayed away from diesel power because of the engine's lack of quick acceleration, its tendency to cause more vibration than gasoline engines, and the relative scarcity of diesel pumps compared to the availability of gas.

However, diesels began to gain favor on the roads of America in the 1970s, particularly in response to an energy crisis that brought skyrocketing pump prices and the first gas rationing since World War II. Volkswagen's new Rabbit diesel enjoyed brisk sales, and General Motors scrambled to bring its own diesel passenger car to the market.

The unfortunate result was the infamous GM diesel, often referred to as the Oldsmobile diesel even though it was marketed through a couple of the General's divisions. Launched in 1978, the engine was eventually the cause of a class-action lawsuit.

A 5.7-liter, 350-cubic-inch unit, the GM diesel engine looked a lot like the gasoline engine of the same size used in similar cars the company made at the time. Some critics say that it was simply that same engine hurriedly converted to run on diesel, though others maintain that it did have the stronger block casting and more robust components needed to withstand the higher compression required for combustion in diesel engines.

GM eventually settled the class-action suit, but the company has not offered a diesel passenger car to Americans since it stopped building the Oldsmobile diesel in 1985.

The GM Diesel is often associated with the now defunct Oldsmobile division, but the infamous engine was also offered to buyers of the Cadillac Seville. It did not succeed as a Cadillac, either.

Some accounts depict the GM diesel as a victim of poor marketing that left many owners unaware of the obstacles of diesel ownership—including limited fuel availability, poor fuel quality, and having to deal with messy pumps and fueling areas.

That said, GM's diesel engine was also plagued by reliability issues. The most troublesome components were head bolts that could not withstand the greater pressures typically required to ignite diesel fuel. Once those gave way, coolant and oil could swap passages—never a good thing for an engine.

While diesel engines remain popular in Europe, fewer than 1 percent of all cars in the United States are powered by the fuel. Though diesel engines are capable of better fuel economy and reliability, and contain fewer moving parts than gasoline engines, they are today found only in some domestic trucks and imported cars. However, concern about both the environment and America's oil supply is prompting a renewed enthusiasm for diesel among the American public, and automakers are taking notice.

In a rushed effort to boost fuel economy in the face of rising gas prices, General Motors introduced its first passenger diesel in 1978. Problems with the engine led to a class action lawsuit, and GM has not offered a diesel-powered car in the United States since.

Trabant

The Trabant, an automobile produced by the East German automaker VEB Sachsenring Automobilwerke Zwickau, was sold in East Germany and other Eastern European socialist countries from 1957 to 1991. The creation of the German Democratic Republic in 1949 had led to a dearth of cars in East Germany. East German citizens could not purchase cars made outside the communist bloc, so VEB Sachsenring, which manufactured tractors and trucks, started making cars to be both sold to the citizens of East Germany, and exported to foreign countries. Two standard Trabant models were offered: the 500, produced until 1963, and the 601, built until 1991, a few years after the fall of the Berlin Wall.

In spite of less than stellar reliability, leisurely performance and other drawbacks, Trabis were popular with car-hungry eastern Europeans, some of whom would wait years for delivery. When the Berlin Wall fell, so did the market for Trabants. In its afterlife, it has developed a cult following among automotive enthusiasts. It has also been incorporated into art installations and music videos.

SPECIFICATIONS

TRABANT P601
Top speed: 68 mph (110 km/h)
0–60 mph (0–97 km/h): 36.8 sec
Engine: Air-cooled, 0.6-liter, two-stroke, two-cylinder engine rated at 27 hp (20 kw) at 4,200 rpm, and 38 lb ft (51 nm) of torque at 3,000 rpm

They were both powered by variants of the same air-cooled 25 horsepower motorcycle engine. In fact, the Trabant was originally designed as a three-wheeled motorcycle powered by this anemic motor. Somewhere during the design process, it was decided that the vehicle should be a four-passenger car, but various components from the motorcycle design were still incorporated into it. Before its introduction, the company dubbed it "Trabant" (German for "satellite") as a tribute to *Sputnik*, the first man-made satellite, which had been launched by the Soviet Union that year.

Unlike cars in Western Europe, which had cleaner four-stroke engines, comfort-

"What do you have when you see a Trabant on the top of a hill? A miracle."

—A COMMON TRABANT JOKE

able cabins, and steel bodies, the Trabi (the Trabant's affectionate nickname, pronounced trah-BEE) was quite austere and used pre-World War II technology. It came in three basic colors: white, blue, and gray.

The Western media often erroneously reported that the Trabant had a cardboard body, due to the lack of steel in East Germany. In truth, most body panels were made with Duroplast, a combination of fabrics such as wool and cotton combined with plastic resins. Though lightweight and inexpensive, Duroplast had its drawbacks for automotive use. It provided poor crash protection, often shattering on impact. Furthermore, it was said that animals such as goats and rats enjoyed feasting on the Trabant's body panels.

The Trabi's power train was even more backward. Oil—mixed with gasoline in the Trabant's fuel tank to lubricate the engine—was burned along with the fuel. The resulting exhaust was a sooty, foul-smelling blue cloud that followed the little car around. Also, the Trabant had no fuel gauge—drivers had to rely on a fuel-tank dipstick to determine their fuel supply.

While the Trabi was trumpeted as a "people's car" by East Germany and other nations behind the Iron Curtain, it was generally ridiculed, even by owners. It was not unknown for buyers to

wait years to take delivery after purchasing. Once put in service, Trabants were unreliable and replacement parts were hard to come by. Owners commonly fashioned their own parts, and a black market for components emerged.

In the late 1980s, *Car and Driver* magazine spoofed the Trabant and even created a parody of rival *Motor Trend* that proclaimed the Trabant the "Auto of the Year." A few years later, after the fall of the Berlin Wall, a Trabant 601 was smuggled into the United States by an East German rock band and given to *Car and Driver* to test. The magazine reported a zero to 60 miles (0–97 km) per hour time of 32.2 seconds and a top speed of 66 miles (106 km) per hour.

When Germany reunified in 1990, many Trabant owners in the former East Germany literally walked away from their Trabants. New-car sales for the Trabant became nonexistent, as buyers preferred even used Western vehicles to the newly inexpensive Trabi. By 1991, production of the Trabant had ended.

Some 15 years after production ceased, the humble Trabant has developed a cult following among European automotive aficionados. Green Trabants, originally designated for military use only, even have some value as a collectible.

Powered by a 25-horse-power, two-stroke engine designed to burn a mixture of gasoline and oil, the Trabant was both smoky and slow.

Yugo

When it comes to bad ideas, it has been reasonably argued that the worst ones involve repeating a mistake somebody else has already made. Doing a lousier job only adds to the pain, but that is basically what automotive entrepreneur Malcolm Bricklin did with the Yugo.

The Eastern European Zastava Corporation built the dated but inexpensively produced automobile under license from the Italian automaker Fiat. Based on a Fiat design from 1971, the Yugo was imported from the former Yugoslavia by Bricklin from the mid-1980s until 1992. Bricklin saw an opportunity to bring a cheap car to American buyers, and to that end he succeeded, with initial pricing at about $4,000—at a time when most entry-level domestic cars cost thousands of dollars more.

SPECIFICATIONS

1990 YUGO CABRIO
Top speed: 93 mph (150 km/h)
0–60 mph (0–97 km/h): 36.8 sec
Engine: 1.3-liter, four-cylinder engine rated at 61 hp (45 kw) at 5,800 rpm, and 68 lb ft (92 nm) of torque at 4,000 rpm

Unfortunately, that is where the fun stopped. Part of the problem was that the Fiat 128, on which the Yugo was based, had already been offered to Americans more than a decade earlier and most had said "No, thanks" the first time. Those who did buy the 128 found themselves the proud owners of a reasonably well-packaged, economically designed car that broke down regularly and had chronic rust problems.

The second time around, Fiat's reincarnated design was subject to more

> "A man walks into an auto parts store and says 'I'd like a gas cap for my Yugo.' 'Okay,' the salesman replies, 'sounds like a fair trade.'"
>
> —A COMMON YUGO JOKE

Based on a Fiat design from 1971, the Yugoslavian-built Yugo was priced thousands of dollars less than any other car sold in the United States when it was introduced in the mid-1980s for about $4,000. This sporty GVS joined the lineup in 1986.

serious issues, as quality control from the Eastern Bloc was even worse than buyers of 128s had come to expect years earlier. However, money talks and memory is short. The Yugo got a lot of press when it was introduced, and the price made it appealing enough that customers were plentiful, with annual sales peaking at 48,812 units.

Four Yugo models were initially offered in the United States. The basic GV (Great Value) was equipped with a 1,100-cc engine and four-speed transmission, and sold for $3,990. Fancier GVL and GVS models had better trim and upholstery. A performance model, the GVX, had a larger, 1,300-cc engine and five-speed

manual transmission, along with alloy wheels and rally lights. A convertible was added in 1988, and if you are looking at a Yugo as part of your retirement portfolio, that would be the one to snap up. One was put into storage when new by an investor, who was recently hoping to fetch more than $20,000 for it. However, the sale was contingent on the car going to a good home—and to an owner with a sense of humor.

A sense of humor is good for any Yugo owner to have, as the chronically unreliable, rust-prone cars have been the butt of jokes in movies, television, and neighborhood garages almost since the first one hit American roads.

Ford Pinto

By the time the 1960s were drawing to a close, "longer, lower, and wider" had been the domestic manufacturers' mantra for a quarter of a century. The largest family cars had grown to a length of almost 20 feet (6.1 m) and weighed in the neighborhood of 5,000 pounds (2,268 kg), often returning gas mileage in the single digits.

Meanwhile, imports had gained a solid foothold in the American market. Sales of Volkswagen Beetles had been growing for 10 years, and European imports including Renault and Fiat had joined the party. Japanese makes were more recent arrivals. The Toyota Corona was the first import to take the quirkiness out of foreign cars—it looked and drove like a miniature domestic sedan. The public went for the Corona in a big way.

The Pinto was rushed into production for the 1971 model year, to compete with economical European and Japanese imports. The price was right at less than $2,000, but the car had serious flaws.

Domestic manufacturers realized that they had to do something—and fast. The Chevrolet Vega and Ford Pinto were rushed to the market, both arriving for the 1971 model year. At a time when the normal development time for a new model was close to four years, the Pinto took just 25 months. Lee Iacocca, development chief who had also been responsible for the wildly successful Mustang, decreed the new small car would not weigh more than 2,000 pounds (907.2 kg) and not cost more

than $2,000. He got both of his wishes, but at no small cost to the company and, sadly, to some unfortunate Pinto buyers and their families.

Like the Vega, the Pinto was plagued with reliability problems, cheesy build quality, and premature rust. The problems with the Pinto did not end there, though. Engineers discovered a design flaw before production began that would prove deadly. In rear-end crash testing, the fuel system ruptured easily, causing horrific fires.

To save weight and meet cost targets, the Pinto's fuel tank had not been properly protected. Worse, it was mounted at the very back of the vehicle, behind the rear axle, where even relatively minor impacts could puncture it. In a rear-ender, the fuel filler could separate from the tank on impact, further increasing the risk of a spill.

Crash tests showed that if a Pinto was hit from behind by a vehicle traveling at over 30 miles (48.3 km) per hour, the car would buckle, the fuel-tank filler would pull out, and gas would immediately begin to leak. At 40 miles (64.4 km) per hour, the results were catastrophic—the collision left the body structure so crumpled that doors were rendered inoperable.

Still, competition was tough, and Ford was losing market share fast. The

It is estimated that between 500 and 900 passengers lost their lives in fiery crashes after being rear-ended in Ford's budget car. This careful driver took matters into her own hands with her 1975 Pinto.

decision was made to put the Pinto into production. The price was $1,995—and potentially serious risk to life and limb.

Because of vigorous lobbying by the Ford Motor Company against government intervention, the National Highway Traffic Safety Administration waited until 1978 to issue a recall on the Pinto.

A 1977 exposé by *Mother Jones* magazine claimed that an estimated 500 to 900 burn deaths could be attributed to the Pinto. A more recent report however, by law professor Gary Schwartz, concluded that far fewer people actually died than originally claimed. Regardless, Ford's decision to knowingly put a defective car into production has made the Pinto an infamous example of callous big-business behavior.

Renault 5 LeCar

French cars have never gained the wide acceptance with buyers in the United States that their manufacturers and designers had hoped for. Generally considered quirky at best, with often-complicated gadgetry and unorthodox styling, they have frequently been described in less flattering terms.

The Renault 5, introduced in Europe in 1972 and later sold in the United States as the LeCar, was a sales success on the east side of the Atlantic from the time of its introduction. Initially offered in Europe as a two-door hatchback with front-wheel drive, the R5 was the best-selling car on the Continent by 1977. The addition of a four-door hatch model in 1979 made it the second best-selling car in the world. According to Renault's Web site, it was the biggest-

selling car in France for more than 10 years and enjoyed numerous racing victories, including the prestigious Monte Carlo rally. Performance variants even included a fire-breathing, mid-engined turbocharged model that retained little of its humble roots.

The Renault 5's European success was so great that the car's American launch was delayed until 1976 because Renault could not meet demand in markets closer to home. With a 1,289-cc engine producing a thrifty and well-intentioned 58 horsepower, the LeCar was well received in the United States when it finally arrived. Despite its compact dimensions, the LeCar offered a remarkably spacious interior with room for four adults, good gas mileage, and a certain continental style. Boosted by

Launched in Europe in 1972, the R5 was such a sales success that Renault could not keep up with demand. As a result, its U.S. debut as the LeCar was delayed until 1976.

In spite of worldwide success, the LeCar is not fondly remembered by many Americans, and has been named to one list of "Worst Cars of the Millennium."

some clever advertising, sales were brisk. The microcar dimensions, combined with the traditionally French cushy ride, and an optional huge folding sunroof, cast the LeCar as an appealing alternative to more ordinary small cars.

In fairness to Renault, the LeCar was a cleverly packaged car that was fun to drive. All cars have come a long way in terms of quality since the 1970s, and some argue the LeCar was no worse than other offerings of the period. In the end, though, the LeCar did little to change the way most Americans had always thought about French cars. The wee Renault was plagued with reliability problems and rust issues that even Americans—who

had stood in lines to buy Chevrolet Vegas—were unwilling to tolerate.

French automakers have since pulled out of the American market. Despite their often remarkably innovative engineering and brisk sales throughout the rest of the world, none of the French companies—not Renault, Citroën, or even Peugeot— sell cars today in the United States.

R5 owners are a devoted and enthusiastic lot, scattered around the globe. In the States, however, the LeCar has ended up on more than one list of famously bad cars, including the nationally syndicated talk-radio show Car Talk's list of the 10 worst cars of the millennium. There, it ranks as number six.

Pontiac Aztek

Despite its ambitious development, Pontiac's first SUV became far more famous for its faults than for its virtues. From build quality that was mediocre at best, to an interior assembled with cheesy plastics, to a disjointed look so ugly that it was hard to believe it was intended, the deck was stacked against the Pontiac Aztek from the moment it hit showrooms as a 2001 model.

Many people, including General Motors Vice Chairman Bob Lutz, believe that GM asked too many people for input in the Aztek's development. From consumer polls to market studies to focus groups, everybody had something to say, and the result was a vehicle that looked like the people responsible for one aspect of its design did not talk to those working on other parts.

Despite unfortunate looks, the Aztek had a versatile, roomy interior with some clever design features. Aimed at a younger, active buyer, the car's emphasis was on utility, with lots of clever storage features, including a center-console mounted removable cooler, along with removable storage boxes and a slide-out load floor. Unlike most other SUVs, the Aztek could swallow up a 4-by-8-foot (1.2 by 2.4 m) sheet of plywood laid flat. Rear seats folded forward, as did the front passenger seat, for transporting really long items. For those so

SPECIFICATIONS

2001 PONTIAC AZTEK
0–60 mph (0–97 km/h): 9.2 sec
Engine: 3.4-liter, V6 engine rated at 185 hp (136 kw) at 5,200 rpm, and 210 ft lb (285 nm) at 4,000 rpm

The Pontiac Aztek could be a poster car exemplifying the hazards of design by committee and focus groups. It is said that the vehicle's developers simply incorporated too many ideas.

merciless in their reviews. The public stayed away in droves, and many Azteks were either sold into rental fleets at discounted prices or assigned to GM executives.

In an effort to stop the bleeding, a slight restyling for 2002 eliminated the ribbed gray plastic cladding that had cloaked the lower third of the body. Replacing the ribbed variety with smoother plastic the same color as the rest of the car helped, but all the cladding in the world could not save the Aztek. Many sat a long time on dealer lots or were heavily discounted to move them.

At least one Aztek owners' club hosts national events, and some Aztek owners truly love their cars. Hopefully they stay happy, because resale values are not good. The Aztek went out of production after the 2005 model year. As of this writing, an Internet search showed a few new ones still available.

As with many panned cars, Aztek owners are a loyal bunch. In fairness to them and the car, Pontiac's first SUV had a versatile interior and plenty of room. Here, it is seen in its 2002 redesign, with uniform cladding.

fond of their Aztek they could not bear to get out of it at the end of the day, a camping package was available, including a tent that attached to the tailgate, an air mattress, and even a twelve-volt air compressor to inflate the mattress.

Based on a minivan platform, the Aztek's odd proportions were partly the result of trying to build a rugged-looking SUV on the underpinnings of the Pontiac Montana. Powered by a 3.4-liter, 185-horsepower V6, both front- or all-wheel drive were available. Offered the first year, a GT package, including larger wheels and more amenities, was quietly dropped for 2002.

General Motors had hoped for as many as 70,000 annual sales with the Aztek, but it sold fewer than half that number during the first year. Its introduction brought howls from the media, who were

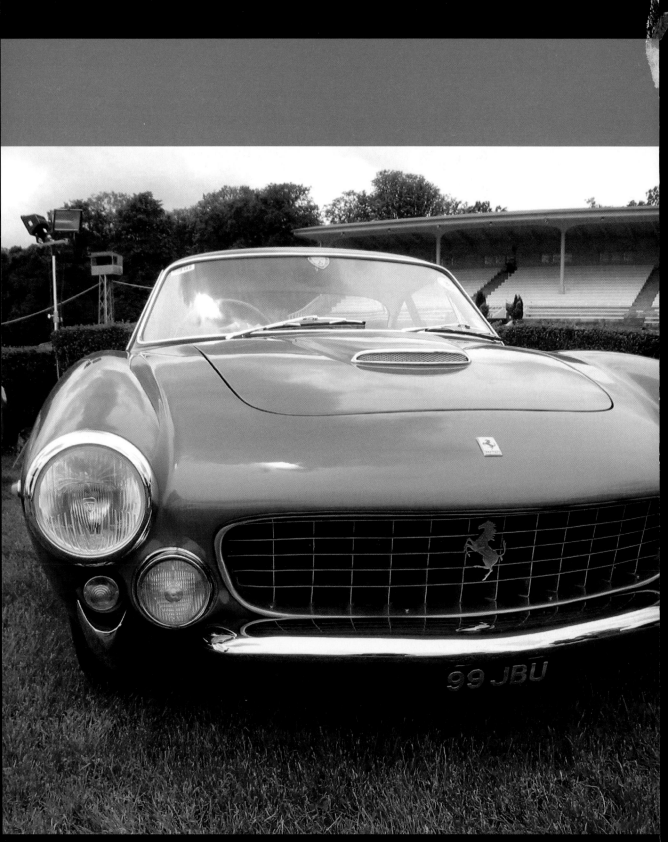

CHAPTER 9

MONEY IS NO OBJECT

THESE ARE CARS THAT INSPIRE SUPERLATIVES. Classic designs since they first spun their tires, these automobiles span the years from the early 20th century to the present day. These are models designed and constructed without compromise for wealthy, discerning buyers, and always in limited numbers.

And they are expensive. Most were far out of the reach of average citizens when new; prices for these sought-after collectibles have risen dramatically in recent years. One, the Bugatti Type 41 Royale, is believed to be the most expensive car ever sold at auction. The imposing Royale was designed by Ettore Bugatti to be the ultimate luxury car—only six were built. No two are alike.

Less imposing, but perhaps more pleasing to look at, is the Ferrari 250 GT Berlinetta Lusso. Ferraris are known for their beauty, but the Lusso is generally regarded as being the most beautiful car ever to wear the Prancing Horse logo.

If one's tastes run to a more modern car in the color of his or her choice, there is always the Maybach—still being sold today. Buyers can choose from enough different paint finishes, leathers, and woods that some two million combinations are available.

Just 350 Ferrari Berlinetta Lussos were produced, with each taking about three months to build. They are regarded as some of the most beautiful Ferraris ever made.

Stutz Bearcat

Harry C. Stutz (1876–1930) started tinkering as a machinist at the age of 18, working at the Davis Sewing Machine Company and at National Cash Register. Four years later, he built his first car, Old Hickory, powered by a two-horsepower engine.

After building and racing a few more designs over the years, becoming chief engineer and designer for the Marion Motor Car Company, and spending some time touring European manufacturers, Stutz entered a car into the inaugural Indianapolis 500 of 1911. This was the first car to bear his name.

The Stutz Bearcat was based on the 1911 Indy car that Harry Stutz had built in a matter of weeks and that Gil Anderson drove to an 11th-place finish.

Five hundred miles later, Gil Anderson, driving the Stutz, had racked up an impressive 11th place finish, with no mechanical problems. Making this even more impressive was the fact the car had been built in just a few weeks. The slogan, "The car that made good in a day" was coined, and the Stutz Motor Car Company was off and running with its Model A (a surprisingly popular name with fledgling car makers in the industry's early days), which was a duplicate of the race car.

The more imaginatively named Bearcat sports car was introduced in 1912. Demand grew so strong that a new plant was constructed in Indianapolis to build it. Low slung and lightweight, the Bearcat was short on creature comforts and did not have doors. With seating for two, the car had a small windscreen that offered the driver a modicum of protection. Powered by a six-cylinder engine, the original Bearcat produced 60 horsepower.

The Bearcat continued to build Stutz's reputation for performance through racing and other competitive events, including a record-breaking coast-to-coast run by race car driver Erwin "Cannonball" Baker in 1915. Mr. Baker (1882–1960) earned his nickname for this drive from San Diego to New York, which took 11 days, seven hours, and 15 minutes without the aid of an interstate system or, for that matter, much pavement.

Part of what made the Bearcat so competitive was its transaxle design, which moved the gearbox to the rear of the car instead of mounting it directly behind the engine. This design, patented by Stutz while at Marion, made for a much more balanced automobile and better handling; this layout is still used by some sports-car designers to this day.

As much as Bearcats were a success on the racetrack, they became a symbol for all that was cool in the roaring twenties. Right up there with a raccoon coat, a Bearcat was a must-have accessory for a young man on the way up in the 1920s.

While Bearcat production continued into the 1920s, in 1916 Stutz sold his interest in the company. He went on to build fire engines and other cars, but none are as widely remembered as the Bearcat. In 2006, a 1914 model sold for a record $715,000 at the Pebble Beach Concours d'Elegance, quite an appreciation from its original $2,000 sale price.

SPECIFICATIONS

1914 STUTZ 4E BEARCAT
Top speed: 75 mph (121 km/h)
Engine: 6.4 liter engine rated at 50 hp (37 kw) at 1,500 rpm

Bottom left: The reliability of the Bearcat engine on the racetrack translated into a sturdy road car.

Bottom right: The Stutz Bearcat was built for performance, with a simple, sturdy cockpit.

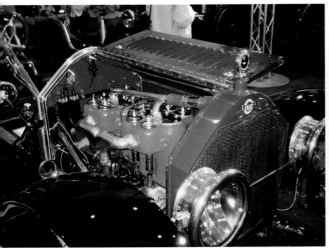

Duesenberg Model J

Right: The Model J was intended to be the finest luxury car in the world. By the time it was ready for production, however, America was in the grips of the Great Depression.

Below: The engineering skills of the Duesenberg brothers enabled them to build cars that won at Indianapolis in 1924, 1925, and 1927. But that did not translate into commercial success, and the Duesenbergs were forced into bankruptcy.

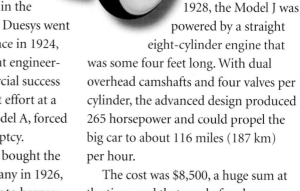

Brothers Fred (1876–1932) and August Duesenberg (1879–1935) set up shop in Des Moines, Iowa, in 1913 with the goal of building sports cars. Self-taught engineers, the Duesenbergs' hand-built designs were considered to be some of the finest auto-mobiles of their time. A Duesenberg finished ninth in the 1913 Indianapolis 500, and Duesys went on to win the prestigious race in 1924, 1925, and 1927. But brilliant engineering did not lead to commercial success for the brothers, whose first effort at a mass-produced car, the Model A, forced their company into bankruptcy.

Entrepreneur E. L. Cord bought the company in 1926, largely to harness the brothers' engineering skills. With a plan to build the finest luxury car in the world, work began on the Model J. First shown as a bare engine and chassis at the New York Automobile Salon in 1928, the Model J was powered by a straight eight-cylinder engine that was some four feet long. With dual overhead camshafts and four valves per cylinder, the advanced design produced 265 horsepower and could propel the big car to about 116 miles (187 km) per hour.

The cost was $8,500, a huge sum at the time, and that was before buyers sprang for coachwork and an interior. Like other luxury cars of the period,

SPECIFICATIONS

1928 DUESENBERG MODEL J
Top speed: 116 mph (186 km/h)
0–60 mph (0–97 km/h): 11 sec
Engine: 6.8 liter in-line eight cylinder engine
    rated at 265 hp (198 kw) at 4,250 rpm

Duesenberg bodies were custom built to a buyer's specifications. A completed Model J would set its well-to-do owner back somewhere between $13,000 and $20,000, depending on its level of extravagance. And this was at a time when a Chevrolet sedan could be had for less than $600, and aspiring homeowners could buy a complete build-it-yourself house kit from Sears for less than $1,000.

Needless to say, the Model J and the supercharged SJ that followed in 1932 never sold in huge numbers, with just 481 built between 1929 and 1937. Owners included actor Clark Gable and the Duke of Windsor, among other wealthy individuals.

Duesenberg closed its doors in 1937, when E. L. Cord's business empire became another victim of the Great Depression. But the Duesenberg legend continued, and decades after the company's demise, noted automotive journalist Ken Purdy wrote in the 1950s that the Model J Duesenberg was "the finest motorcar yet built in the United States."

Duesenberg automobiles are still admired for their unique engineering and style, and most of the Model J and SJ Duesys built still exist today. Largely residing in climate-controlled garages or museums, they are prized by collectors. And their prices still put them out

GM FUTURLINER BUS

The most expensive American-made vehicle ever sold at auction is not a thoroughbred race car nor is it a hand-built, ultrarare exotic. It is a bus. A General Motors Futurliner show bus, to be exact, one of 12 the carmaker manufactured in the early 1940s for its "Parade of Progress" road show. The show was begun in 1936 as a way for GM to take its World's Fair exhibit and vehicle lineup to the masses. Repeated again in the early 1940s and the early 1950s, all included Futurliners, which opened up to display exhibits. None were ever put into service carrying passengers.

Tall and imposing, the Futurliner looks as much like a locomotive as a road-going vehicle, and is a rolling testament to the optimism of its time. The driver sits with his or her head about 11 feet above the roadway and accesses the center-mounted cockpit by using a stairway. From there, one witnesses a commanding, if relaxed, view of the countryside while touring at a top speed of 40 miles (64.4 km) per hour. The Futurliner famously sold at auction in 2006 was the 11th built, and one of the last surviving examples. The price? $4,320,000.

of the reach of most Sears homeowners, with Duesenbergs now trading for millions of dollars.

Painstakingly restored, Futurliner number 10 belongs to the National Automotive and Truck Museum of the United States.

Bugatti Type 41 Royale

Truly a piece of personal transportation for the person who has at least one of everything, the Bugatti Royale is all about excess. For starters, there is the engine. With 12.7 liters of displacement, which works out to 700 cubic inches, the inline eight-cylinder engine contained in the Royale was about twice the size of most V8s employed by American carmakers in the later glory days of the

V8. The single-overhead-cam design produced about 300 horsepower, and it remains the largest engine ever designed for use in a passenger car built for public consumption. Ettore Bugatti (1881–1947) was expecting a contract to build 16-cylinder aircraft engines for the French military in the 1920s and had began development work on the engine. When the deal never materialized, incorporating one of the banks of cylinders—roughly half the engine—seemed to Ettore like a dandy way to power his flagship mega-luxury car.

And mega it was. The wheelbase was a little over 14 feet (4.3 m) long, and Royales stood as much as five feet tall at the hood, depending on the body chosen by the buyer. Its wheels were some two feet in diameter. The cars weighed in the neighborhood of 7,000 pounds (3,175 kg). To put it in perspective, the Royale weighed a little less than three new 2007 Honda Fit hatchbacks.

Body styles included limousines, coupes, and open cars, and no two were alike. One roadster built for a successful clothing manufacturer was styled by Jean Bugatti, the promising son of the company's founder. The buyer specified a design without headlights so as not to interrupt the flowing lines of the car. Apparently he had no plans to drive at night.

SPECIFICATIONS

1930 BUGATTI TYPE 41 ROYALE
Top speed: 100 mph (160 km/h)
Engine: Twin spark in-line eight cylinder engine rated at 300 hp (193 kw) at 1,700 rpm

This Kellner-bodied Bugatti Royale sold for 5.5 million pounds at a 1987 Christie's auction in London. That works out to about $8,700,000 at the time, making it the most expensive car ever sold.

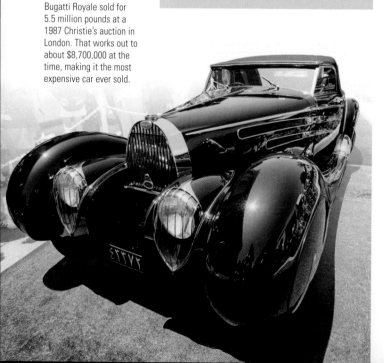

Left: Only ten examples of the Bugatti Royale were built. No two are alike. This Royale is in the Schlumpf Collection at the Cité de l'Automobile National Museum in France.

Below: The massive wheels of the Bugatti Royale measure 24 inches (61 cm) in diameter.

Timing is everything, and one thing the world did not need at the onset of the Great Depression in 1930 was the world's most imposing luxury car. In 1931, a bare Royale chassis and engine cost about $25,000, a princely sum at the time. Once fitted with bodywork and an interior, a completed Royale cost in the neighborhood of $40,000, depending on the buyer's desires. Just 10 Royales were built during a production run that began in 1927 and ended in 1933. Two of the 10 stayed within the Bugatti estate for many years.

Royales have occupied the very top of the collector car market for years, breaking records on the infrequent occasions when one of the 10 comes up for sale. One bodied by coachbuilder Kellner Royale sold for £5.5 million at a 1987 Christie's auction in London, which was roughly $8,700,000 at the time. The same car was later said to have been sold to a Japanese concern for a reported $15,800,000, but details get sketchy high in the rarefied air.

Mr. Bugatti's flagship may not have been much of a commercial success in his time, but its legend is alive and well today.

Ferrari 250 GT Lusso Berlinetta

Enzo Ferrari (1898–1988), it is often said, built and sold road cars only as a means to support his company's racing efforts. The 250 GT Lusso is an example of one such car. Regarded by some Ferraristi as being the most beautiful Ferrari ever built, the Lusso of 1963–64 was last in a series of 14 3.0-liter, V12-powered, 250-series cars built in the 1950s and '60s. These iconic cars were successful on tracks all over the world. Using one, Ferrari entered and won its first World Sports Car Manufacturers Championship in 1953, returning to repeat victories in 1954, 1956, 1957, and 1958.

Unveiled at the Paris Motor Show in October 1962, with all-new styling and a more luxurious interior, the Lusso was intended from the start to be a road car. Just 350 were produced, with each taking about three months to build. Lusso bodies were made primar-

SPECIFICATIONS

1964 FERRARI 250 GT LUSSO BERLINETTA
0–60 mph (0–97 km/h): 8 sec
1/4 mile (0.4 km): 16.1 sec
Engine: 3 liter V12 engine rated at 250 hp (184 kw) at 7,500 rpm, and 215 lb ft (291 nm) of torque at 5,500 rpm

ily of steel, with aluminum used for the doors, hood, and trunk.

Pininfarina designed the timeless lines of the exterior. The Italian firm founded by Battista "Pinin" Farina in 1930 has been responsible for the look of many Ferraris since the 1950s; it is a relationship that continues today. Coachbuilder Scaglietti translated Pininfarina's design into reality.

Often described as being voluptuous, a description of any mechanical device some might find curious, it is hard to dispute that the Lusso is a gorgeous design. *Car and Driver* magazine described the Lusso in its May 1964 issue as being so beautiful that "its proportions approach perfection." Inside, the cabin is light and airy, with excellent visibility aided by large windows and thin roof pillars. Good visibility is key in a 150-mile (241.4 km) per hour car that wears no exterior rearview mirrors to break up its smooth lines.

But beauty goes further than skin deep with the Lusso, whose engine and

The large rear window of the Lusso tapered to very thin roof pillars, giving the interior an open, airy ambiance.

tubular space frame were adapted from the 250 GTO and 250 GT/SWB (for short wheelbase) racing cars. The Lusso is powered by a slightly milder version of the V12 than the one used in its racing relatives. In Berlinetta form, the engine has three carburetors in place of the racing version's six and delivers about 250 horsepower. With a four-speed manual transmission, four-wheel disc brakes, and a comfortable cockpit with leather seating for two, the Lusso makes an exceptional grand tourer.

One of the customers to snap one up was actor and car enthusiast Steve McQueen, well known for his roles in the legendary gearhead movies *Bullitt* and *LeMans*. He and his wife were so taken by their Lusso that they embarked on a 1,500-mile (2,141 km) road trip in it shortly after purchasing the car. McQueen, who collected, bought, and sold many cars during his lifetime, is believed to have kept his Lusso until 1973. Today, McQueen's car is worth somewhere north of $400,000; one Lusso with a racing pedigree sold for just under $600,000 in late 2006. Not bad for a car that cost a bit more than $13,000 new.

Though Ferraris are known for being red, the Lusso came in many colors, including black, green, red, and brown.

Mercedes-Benz 600 Pullman

Originally appearing at the Frankfurt Motor Show of 1963, the Mercedes 600 sedan spent two more years in development before going into production as the German carmaker's top-of-the-line model—a position it held through 1981. In all those years, just 2,677 of the hand-built, special-order models were constructed, most then serving duty shuttling world leaders and dignitaries. Some were heavily armored from the factory—so heavily that rear doors were hydraulically operated and opened with the push of a button.

The crème de la crème of these were the long-wheelbase versions built with either four or six doors. Roughly 450 models were constructed, and designated Pullman. They featured hydraulically

powered seats, windows, and a sound-proof divider to keep the driver from listening in on high-level negotiations. Rarer still are one-third landau and two-thirds Presidential convertible models, suitable only for the bravest politicos. These had convertible roofs covering part of the rear passenger compartment.

One Pullman was sold to Charles Schulz, creator of the comic strip *Peanuts*, who picked the car up in Germany for a European road trip before shipping it home. Equipped with

Entertainers, cartoonists, and world leaders were all seduced by the solidity and opulence of the Mercedes-Benz 600 Pullman. This one is now in the collection of the Mercedes-Benz Museum in Stuttgart, Germany.

SPECIFICATIONS

1964 MERCEDES-BENZ 600 PULLMAN
Top speed: 127 mph (205 km/h)
0–60 mph (0–97 km/h): 9.7 sec
Engine: 6.3 liter V8 engine rated at 247 hp (184 kw) at 4,000 rpm, and 369 lb ft (500 nm) of torque at 2,800 rpm

the front fender–mounted flag holders that were popular options for heads of state, Schulz's car flew a Snoopy flag from one, and a Red Baron flag from the other. His car is also believed to be the only left-hand-drive 600 Pullman ordered in bright Signal Red. Driving a bright red, mammoth Mercedes limousine with flags fluttering from the front fenders, no doubt Mr. Schulz was plenty conspicuous.

Pullmans were not just hand-built, they were built in a completely separate factory from other Mercedes-Benz models by some of the carmaker's most experienced and skilled craftsmen. The first production Mercedes equipped with a modern V8, the 600 utilized a 6.3-liter engine producing 247 horsepower. That was enough to propel the hefty 7,000-pound (3,175 kg), seven-passenger model to a top speed of close to 130 miles (209.2 km) per hour. To help keep comfy both the world leaders and notorious despots who favored the 600 for personal transportation, all models were equipped with an air suspension.

Chairman Mao is said to have been the proud owner of 23 600s. Idi Amin had a humble three. The Vatican parking garage contained just one, but Elvis Presley and Hugh Hefner reportedly had two each.

Because production continued for so many years and many 600s were well maintained while traveling relatively few miles, you can probably find one in good shape. But they are not cheap, and the hydraulics can be expensive to maintain. And if your taste runs to a big, red Pullman formerly owned by a well-known cartoonist, think seven figures. At least you could save money by supplying your own fender flags.

During a production run that lasted until 1981, almost 20 years, only about 450 handcrafted 600 Pullman models were built in a factory of their own.

Maybach

Car shoppers looking for a Maybach can go to the company Web site to find a retail outlet, just like buyers of more mundane Chevrolets or Toyotas. However, rather than being directed to a dealership after typing in their zip code, Maybach shoppers are guided to a "studio." The same site offers the option of symphonic music or no symphonic music. Alternatively, a prospective customer can reach a Maybach Relationship Manager by calling a toll-free number. Things are a little different when you are playing in the big leagues.

Born of a desire to provide its highest-end customers with something to aspire to beyond a mere Mercedes S600, DaimlerChrysler brought back a name from its own history books when it announced the Maybach in 1998.

Wilhelm Maybach (1846–1929) was an early automotive engineer, designer, and pioneer, who along with his son Karl produced some of the finest luxury cars of the 1920s and 1930s. After his start as a

protégé of Gottlieb Daimler, Wilhelm is credited as the designer of the first Mercedes in 1900, a 35-horsepower model with an all-alloy engine.

Marketing cars built under his own name beginning in 1921, Maybach built high-quality, low-production models with innovative designs and engines as large as eight liters and 12 cylinders. The Type DS 8 Zeppelin, a 12-cylinder roadster built in the '30s, developed 200 horsepower and rode on a 12-foot wheelbase. Some 200 DS 8 Zeppelins were built, and only about 1,800 Maybachs were built in all.

The modern Maybach is meant to capture more than a little of the spirit of the original. Available only in a four-door sedan body style, buyers can choose from either the 18.8-foot- (5.7 m) long model 57, or the 20.24-foot- (6.2 m) long 62. Either one provides a hushed, spacious, and smooth ride.

Largely hand-built in Sindelfingen, Germany, each Maybach could take up to four weeks to construct. The plant employs just over 300 skilled workers, with a sales goal of no more than 1,000 cars per year.

Power comes from a twin-turbo, aluminum and magnesium 5.5-liter, V12 engine producing 550 horsepower and an even more impressive 663 pound-feet of torque. The big engine provides sufficient motivation to propel the hefty sedan from 0–62 (0–100 km) per hour in just 5.4 seconds. If that is not fast enough, a 6.0-liter V12 good for 604 horsepower is also available. Either is matched with a five-speed automatic transmission.

Inside, the opulent interior features an electro-transparent, panoramic glass roof that passengers can make clear or opaque at their whim. Buyers can choose from a variety of woods,

leathers, and paint finishes, for a combination of some two million design alternatives. This assures that each Maybach is unique and that designers like Henry Ford and Alec Issigonis would not approve.

With Maybach prices ranging from $335,000 to $426,000, one has to wonder how anyone in the financial position to consider a Maybach would have the time for those two million decisions. Maybe they just hire somebody to make them.

SPECIFICATIONS

2006 MAYBACH 62
Top speed: 155 mph (250 km/h)
0–62 mph (0–100 km/h): 5.4 sec
Engine: 5.5 liter V12 engine rated at 550 hp (410 kw) at 5,250 rpm, and 663 lb ft (898 nm) of torque at 2,300 rpm

The building of a new Maybach can take up to four weeks. Each is largely hand assembled, and the plant where they are constructed employs just over 300 workers, with a sales goal of no more than 1,000 cars per year.

CAR PEOPLE PART 2

CHAPTER 10

CARS OF THE RICH AND THE INFAMOUS

IT IS, INDEED, A WORLD ON WHEELS. We all travel by car—ordinary citizens, heads of state, refugees, religious dignitaries—even cult leaders. Most of us choose our vehicles based on individual needs and tastes, including the rich, famous, and infamous among us, whose tastes can be a bit different from those of the people next door.

Less concerned with the mundane, like how many bags of groceries can fit in the trunk or how good the gas mileage is, some seek vehicles that can shield them from assassination or enable them to wave to crowds of admirers in subtropical heat while rolling along in air-conditioned comfort. Others may seek a truck capable of a treacherous, 90-mile (145 km), open-water exodus from the rule of a dictator.

Fortunately, vehicles are available to meet these needs or have been adapted to do so. After all, the rich, famous, and infamous share at least one basic necessity with the rest of us: They have places to go.

Left: President Bill Clinton's Cadillac limousine is conspicuous as it arrives at a 1994 G7 summit in Detroit. Inset: In 2003, 12 Cuban migrants were interdicted while rumbling to America in their infamous 1951 Chevy truck/ boat. The migrants were deported to Cuba, but they returned to drive the Florida Straits again roughly a year later. Pages 148–149: Race car driver Danica Patrick is mobbed by photographers after a race.

Head of State Limos

Powerful people tend to favor powerful cars. Leaders of nations are, generally speaking, powerful people. Depending on the nation though, some are more powerful than others.

Whenever possible, these leaders prefer to ride in automobiles produced in their own countries—which makes solid business sense and is good for morale. It cannot hurt at election time, either.

For everybody else, there is always Mercedes-Benz. At least that used to be the case; other automakers, including BMW, Audi, and Volkswagen, have been stealing some of Mercedes's fire of late, as well as its reputation for building rock-solid, armored limos. Egyptian president Mohamed Hosni Mubarak prefers

Queen Elizabeth II's 2002 Bentley State Limousine is heavily armored, and has a top speed of 130 miles (209.2 km) per hour. There are only two of these cars in existence, both belonging to the queen.

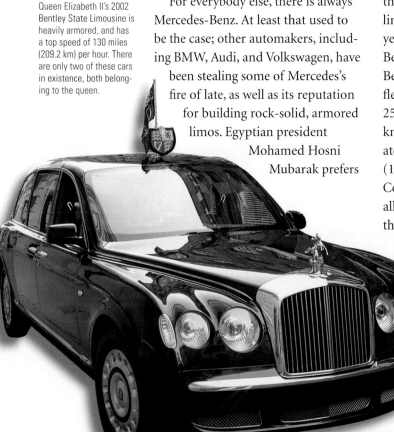

a BMW 7-Series Protection; the king of Spain rides in an Audi A8 Security. Even German chancellor Angela Merkel has ditched Mercedes-Benz in favor of an Armored Volkswagen Phaeton. At least she stuck with a German car.

British royals have preferred Rolls-Royces for years, as is only appropriate. However, in 2002 the queen of England showed her willingness to try something new, accepting the gift of a custom-made Bentley limo in honor of her Golden Jubilee year. Taking two years to build, the Bentley state limousine was the first Bentley to enter service in the royal fleet. Designed to last a minimum of 25 years and 125,000 miles (201,168 km), the Bentley is expected to operate at an average speed of nine miles (15 km) per hour for most of its life. Considering that the queen occasionally uses another car or two, one would think the Bentley has a more-than-likely shot at meeting its designers' longevity goals, assuming that it does not collapse under its own bulk. It tips the scales at 7,474 pounds (3,390 kg).

George W. Bush, on the other hand and the other side of the pond, rides in a stretched and armored 2006 Cadillac DTS, which was delivered brand new just in time for the inauguration ceremony marking his second term as U.S. president on January 20, 2005. Bush was actually the first citizen to take delivery of any 2006 DTS—the civilian version was not officially shown to the public until the Chicago Auto Show the following month. Not that Mr. Bush's hand-built DTS has all that much in common with anything available at your local dealer. Longer, wider, and taller than Cadillac's production model, the presidential limousine is equipped with a customized interior including adaptive seats that sense the position of occupants and adjust the cushion accordingly.

Meanwhile, Mercedes-Benz is preparing a worldwide campaign to try and regain its position as the premier choice of premiers. The company is currently developing a new, stretched version of its top-of-the-line S600 sedan that will feature all the comforts of a leather-lined, and heavily armored mobile office. Powered by a 5.5-liter, 517-horsepower 12-cylinder engine with twin turbochargers, standard equipment will include run-flat tires and a self-sealing fuel tank. As far as the option list is concerned, Mercedes-Benz says: "Even the most unusual of customer requests can be met."

Secret Service agents flank President George W. Bush's 2006 Cadillac DTS limousine during the president's 2005 inaugural parade.

Refugee Chevy

Cubans living under the regime of Fidel Castro are nothing if not an improvisational bunch. Since Castro came to power in 1959, residents of the island nation have learned how to keep their automobiles running with baling wire and/or whatever else they can scrounge up.

American cars were once common on the island, but when trade relations with the United States ended, imports of Fords, Chevrolets, and other Detroit iron also ceased, along with supplies of parts to maintain them. The stock of replacement components dried up quickly, and enterprising Cubans with some mechanical ability, in addition to making their own replacement parts, resorted to adapting parts from Russian-built vehicles to keep their aging Chevys on the road.

Among Cubans who opted to leave their homeland for the United States during Castro's reign, backyard mechanical ingenuity has helped many to successfully brave the Florida Straits, an often-treacherous, 90-mile (145 km) passage separating Cuba and the Florida Keys. Most *balseros* ("rafters") emigrated by raft or boat, but others bravely set out in those old American automobiles adapted to float.

Childhood friends Luis Grass and Marcial Basanta may be some of the most enterprising emigrants ever to attempt such a crossing. If nothing else, theirs were some of the most well-publicized attempts. Grass, a mechanical engineer by trade, had eked out a living in Havana for years, using his 1951 Chevrolet truck for odd jobs. That ended when the government confiscated the truck. Shortly thereafter, Grass, who still had a spare key to the Chevy, drew up plans to make one more run with his beloved truck.

The United States Coast Guard took this photo of the truckonauts—as they came to be known—prior to interdicting the group and sinking the truck. Luis Grass was at the wheel, and the group planned to just drive up the beach and hit the road when they reached the Florida shore.

"In life you have to set goals. Whoever lives in fear doesn't deserve to live."

—LUIS GRASS

After "borrowing" the truck back, Grass and Basanta scrounged up sheet metal and other parts on the black market, and with the aid of trusted friends discreetly converted the Chevy into an oceangoing vehicle. They welded metal to its bottom to make it watertight, and fitted a propeller driven by the driveshaft. A pointed prow was fabricated to help the two-ton flatbed slice through the sea, and six 55-gallon (208.2 l) drums surrounding the truck added buoyancy. Power came from the original, 50-year-old, 236-cubic-inch, six-cylinder engine.

In July 2003, Luis and Marcial set out for Florida with 10 other friends and family members. They did not reach the American coast, but it was neither the fault of their engineering nor because of the ancient truck, which performed beautifully, considering that it was never intended to be pressed into service as a boat decades after it was built. In a widely publicized case, the truck soldiered on until it was about 40 miles (64.4 km) from the Florida Keys. The U.S. Coast Guard then intercepted the truck, and safely removed its occupants before unceremoniously shooting out the barrels that kept it afloat.

Basanta and Grass were returned to Cuba, as is United States policy for Cuban refugees interdicted before reaching U.S. shores. They did not give up, though. In 2004, they tried again in a remarkably clean-looking, modified '59 Buick four-door, which was, according to Grass, an improvement over the truck. Photographs of the Balseros cruising across the straits with their arms on the windowsills made it look like they were just out for a Sunday drive.

Sadly for the childhood friends, the Coast Guard was once again waiting, and their second ingenious vehicle was intercepted, though Grass claims that it was not sunk and may still exist. Basanta remains in Cuba, but Grass and his family eventually made it to the United States, traveling overland from Costa Rica. Grass now works in a southern Florida General Motors dealership. Odds are you could not find a better guy to keep your Chevy on the road—or above water.

Luis Grass, left, Marcial Basanta, center, and Ariel Diego talk with journalists in Havana, Cuba, in 2003. All three were aboard the 1951 Chevy truck/boat, which was intercepted 40 miles (64.4 km) from the Florida coast. Grass eventually made it to the United States—traveling overland, however, through Central America and across the Mexican border.

Popemobile

For decades, motor vehicles have been used around the world to provide the faithful with a glimpse of the Holy Father long before the term *Popemobile* came into popular use.

Since an assassination attempt on John Paul II in 1981, the preferred transportation for the pope's public motor cruises has been a vehicle with a distinctive, bulletproof-glass booth on the back, tall enough for the pontiff to stand in and wave at crowds. Since then, any vehicle that has ever carried the pope has been described as a Popemobile, even if it was built 50 years before the assault. The term has been applied to a number of unique pope-carrying cars, trucks, and SUVs over the years.

Pope Benedict XVI waves from his Mercedes-Benz Popemobile while visiting his homeland of Germany.

SPECIFICATIONS

1980 MERCEDES-BENZ 230 G POPEMOBILE
Top speed: 81 mph (130.4 km/h)
Engine: Four-cylinder engine rated at 100 hp (74 kw) at 5,200 rpm

Many have been Mercedes-Benz models, going back to 1930 when Pope Pius XI first climbed into a Nürburg 460 limousine—a gift of the German carmaker. Mercedes-Benz has continued to supply a number of Popemobiles ever since, including sedans, limos, and more modern, bulletproof SUVs equipped with all-wheel drive and the phone booth-esque compartment on the back enabling huge crowds to get a glimpse as the pope rolls by.

For the pope's comfort and security, the current Popemobile is equipped not only with bulletproof Plexiglas, but with handrails for extra grip on rough roads and air conditioning potent enough to cool the booth in tropical heat. Handgrips and capable air conditioning are as important to the Popemobile as shoulder harnesses and airbags are to regular cars, especially when crawling along unpaved roads in third-world countries at 10 miles (16 km) per hour.

In the Americas, one notable Popemobile was a Lehman-Peterson Lincoln conversion limousine used

by Pope Paul VI during a 1965 visit to New York. That vehicle was later used by President Lyndon Baines Johnson and also saw duty as an astronaut parade vehicle. The Lincoln was lengthened by some 20 inches (51 cm) more than a stock Continental and equipped with an open roof over the rear section of the passenger compartment. The pope's seat could be raised 13 inches (33 cm) to allow crowds a better view of His Holiness, and a second windshield was mounted atop the forward section of the roof to add extra protection when the seat was raised.

For one 1984 visit to Canada, two Popemobiles based on Chevrolet pickups were built in a facility near Montreal. That way, to keep up with the pope's tight schedule, one Popemobile could be advanced to the next city on his tour while he puttered along in the

Pope Paul VI famously used this 1964 Lincoln while visiting New York. It featured a mechanically rising seat that could elevate the pope if he grew tired of standing.

other one at an average speed of nine miles (15 km) per hour.

In recent years, the most popular Popemobile has been a Mercedes-Benz ML SUV for public appearances, but the late Pope John Paul II is said to have had a taste for SUVs from a number of makers. Apparently, his truly favorite ride around town was an older limo inherited from a previous pontiff. Surely, he found it nice to ride around for once without having to stand up.

A DIFFERENT KIND OF POPEMOBILE

In 2005, a humble Volkswagen Golf sold on eBay for about 189,000 euros, which was about $244,000 at the time. The 1999 Golf had only 47,000 miles on the odometer, but that was not what brought such a staggering sale price. Paperwork for the car suggested that one of the Golf's previous owners was Cardinal Joseph Ratzinger, known these days as Pope Benedict XVI.

During the 10-day auction, some 8.4 million visitors to eBay viewed the Golf. Bids skyrocketed as the auction drew to a close, and the price of the car doubled during the last 24 hours.

In the end, the winner was a Texas casino that already boasted ownership rights to a number of novelty pop-culture and religious artifacts. The casino recently auctioned the car again on eBay. It is anyone's guess where the holy roller will end up next.

David Koresh's Cars

David Koresh, as seen in a 1988 police line-up photo. At the time, Koresh was fighting for control of the Branch Davidians.

David Koresh was the leader of the Branch Davidians, a religious sect located outside of Waco, Texas, in the early 1990s. In 1993, four agents of the Bureau of Alcohol, Tobacco, and Firearms (ATF) were shot and killed when they attempted to arrest Koresh on weapons charges. The government then laid siege to the heavily armed Branch Davidian compound and attempted to negotiate surrender with Koresh. The 51-day standoff between the Branch Davidians and a team of FBI and ATF agents ended when the compound burned to the ground during a botched raid on April 19, 1993. Some 80 cult members, including Koresh, perished during the initial standoff and the fire that ensued.

Besides guns, and other unmentionables, Koresh had a taste for fast automobiles. He and some of his followers enjoyed tinkering with cars and motorcycles, most of which were destroyed during the siege and raid. As seen in transcripts of Koresh's negotiations with federal authorities, as cool as he remained during the siege, he became notably upset and emotional when the Feds damaged or destroyed vehicles parked outside the compound.

The cryptic message that David Koresh stamped into his Camaro's 427-cubic-inch (6,997-cu. cm.) V8 engine block.

One such vehicle was a restored 1968 Chevrolet El Camino owned by cult member Paul Fatta. The El Camino was a pickup truck/car combination made by Chevrolet from the 1950s to the 1980s. Fatta's was an SS-396 high-performance model that he apparently spent thousands of dollars restoring. However, it depreciated rapidly after being crushed by a tank.

A car owned by Koresh was also damaged during the siege, but was not destroyed. Described as his daily driver, Koresh's black 1968 Chevrolet Camaro had been modified with custom wheels and tires, and a monster, 500-horsepower, 427-cubic-inch V8 engine matched with a four-speed manual transmission. Koresh had also stamped the words "Davides 427 Go God" into the engine block.

Long after the siege, the Camaro was sold to the owner of an auto parts store. The car was later sold again, and the new owner repaired some of the body damage before parking it outside his garage for eight years. Apparently, it was not his number-one project. Finally, the Camaro was sold to a more opportunistic owner who restored it with an engine rebuild, new tires, and a fresh coat of black paint. He then auctioned it in 2004, complete with a title listing David Koresh as the owner.

Despite many bidders being understandably put off by the car's history, the Camaro brought $37,000—more than twice the price of several other vintage Camaros sold at the same auction. The seller had been angling for more like $80,000, but clearly the karma, if not the car, was too pricey for most people.

The extensive damage to Bonnie and Clyde's '32 Ford is visible in this period press photo. Clyde Barrow was apparently fond of the Ford V8 engine and favored Fords as getaway cars.

BONNIE AND CLYDE'S '32 FORD

Bonnie Parker and Clyde Barrow may well be the most famous gangsters from those Depression-era days when robbing banks was fashionable in certain circles. It is at least fair to say that they are the most well-known lovebirds on the wrong side of the law—a romantic team who drove around the heartland stealing money and cars, and outrunning and outgunning law-enforcement officials.

It was in one of their stolen cars that Mr. Barrow and Ms. Parker met their end on the morning of May 23, 1934, shortly after stopping for sandwiches in Gibsland, Louisiana. According to some accounts, Bonnie was still holding her partly eaten sandwich after a posse of police from both Lousiana and Texas pumped some 130 rounds into their stolen '32 Ford.

Barrow was apparently a big fan of the newly introduced 1932 Ford, which was powered by a flathead V8 that later became a favorite of customizers and hot rodders. He stole several of them during his short career, and the Henry Ford Museum contains a letter to Henry Ford, signed by Barrow, singing the praises of the V8 engine.

CHAPTER 11

COLLECTORS AND
THEIR COLLECTIONS

FOR SOME CAR ENTHUSIASTS, having one or two prized vehicles to tinker with and roll out on the weekend is enough to keep them interested, busy, and always on the verge of financial crisis. For others with enough money, storage space, and time, the stakes get higher—although financial crisis remains a possibility for anybody involved in car collecting.

Like any habit, it is possible to get hooked, and collectors will tell you that one car in their possession leads to another, and another, and another. Once you have gotten to 10 or 12, why not buy a couple more?

In this chapter, we look at some serious collectors and their collections—some of which total thousands of cars, as well as other motor vehicles. Each collection is as much a reflection of its owner as it is a bunch of things on wheels and related memorabilia. Some go for racing cars, some go for classics, and some just follow their interests, buying what they like.

Liberace poses with a 1956 Rolls Royce Silver Cloud I. He used the automobile during a show at Radio City Music Hall in 1985. The flamboyant entertainer often utilized cars from his unique collection as stage props in his shows.

Howard Hughes

Born on Christmas Eve in 1905, Howard Robard Hughes (1905–76) was an orphan by age 18. Hughes, an only child, inherited an estate worth $871,000, along with the patent for a drill bit used for most oil and gas drilling at the time. Manufactured exclusively by the family-owned Hughes Tool Company, the drill bit brought in a steady stream of revenue. After his father died, Hughes left school to take control of the company.

Young Hughes's interests went far beyond drill bits, however profitable they were. He went on to become a movie producer, aviation pioneer, and car collector. Although his may not have been the largest collection, the cars he chose reflected the personality of the man and his idiosyncrasies.

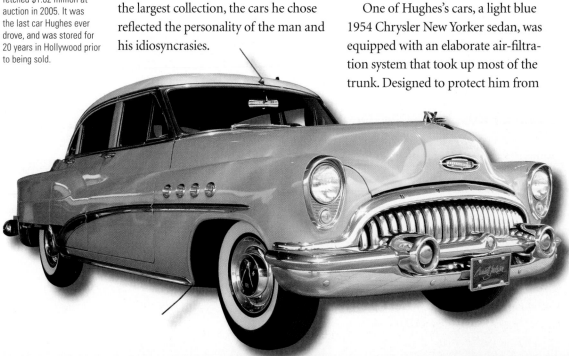

Hughes had a fear of infection that he may have inherited from his mother, who went to great lengths to protect her only son from germs. Eventually Hughes became a paranoid recluse, rarely seen in public during the last years of his life.

One of Hughes's cars, a light blue 1954 Chrysler New Yorker sedan, was equipped with an elaborate air-filtration system that took up most of the trunk. Designed to protect him from

> "I'm not a paranoid, deranged millionaire. Goddamit, I'm a billionaire."
>
> —HOWARD HUGHES

SPECIFICATIONS

HOWARD HUGHES
Size of collection: More than 125 cars
Notable cars: 1953 Buick Roadmaster sedan,
   1954 Chrysler New Yorker sedan, 1956 Ford
   Thunderbird convertible

bacteria, it also supplemented the car's factory air conditioning, something even a non-germophobe would want in Hughes's hometown of Las Vegas. Still, Hughes apparently had little confidence in the system's efficacy. When the car was offered for sale in 2005, it showed fewer than 2,000 miles on the odometer. Complete with filtration system, the car was advertised for $125,000.

Another Hughes car of note is a 1956 Ford Thunderbird convertible, used as a chase car for a 1959 world record run for the longest continuous flight by an aircraft. After a Cessna 172 took off from Las Vegas and stayed aloft for 64 days, refueling in the air, the pilots would swoop low to get food and water from the speeding Thunderbird. The record still stands; the T-Bird sold at auction in 2006 for $86,400.

Despite his near-pathological fear of infection, Hughes bought a number of open cars—though he did not ride in them very often, it seems. His collection included a powder blue 1957 Chrysler Imperial convertible, rumored to have been purchased for one of his girlfriends. With low miles, it sold for $378,000 at the same auction as the Thunderbird.

The most extraordinary price paid for a Hughes vehicle was the $1.62 million brought by his 1953 Buick Roadmaster four-door sedan in 2005. Like the Chrysler, it was equipped with an air-filtration system mounted in the trunk. Hughes had also retrofitted it with a 24-volt electrical system that he could use to start (with connector cables) his own airplane, thus keeping him one step ahead of all those he believed were following him with ill-intent.

Howard Hughes played many roles in his lifetime—blockbuster movie producer, record-breaking pilot, and, of course, car collector. By the end of his life, Hughes was most famous for his reclusive, paranoid lifestyle and his germophobia. The automobiles he used reflect both the daring and fearful aspects of his personality.

William Harrah

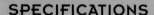

Bottom left: The National Automobile Museum, which was founded using Harrah's collection, situates its cars in contemporary scenes. The 1930s street exhibit advertises *Gone with the Wind* on the theater marquee; a line of thirties-era cars is parked out front.

Bottom right: Among the collection at the National Automobile Museum is a 1934 Dymaxion, designed by R. Buckminster Fuller. The unique automobile was three-wheeled; it used its single rear wheel as a rudder. Fuller had big plans for the Dymaxion as an economic people mover—the car could reach 120 miles (193 km) per hour with a fuel economy nearing 30 miles per gallon (12.74 km/l). Unfortunately for Fuller, he was never able to make the Dymaxion a mass-produced reality.

Gambling and hotel mogul William Fisk Harrah (1911–78) exemplified living large. The empire he started building as a young man when he bought a gambling operation from his father for $500 in 1933 continued to grow until his death in 1978. By that time, his casinos were an institution—Harrah's was the first casino company to be listed on the New York Stock Exchange.

An avid car collector for many years, Harrah went large with his automobiles as well. By the time of his death, he had amassed a collection of some 1,500 automobiles. As the head of a company with the slogan "Live it up," Harrah clearly knew how to set an example.

The exact number in the collection is

hard to pin down; what is known is that the man who once vowed to have an example of every car his family owned during his childhood ended up not only with those sentimental pieces, but an immense and incredibly broad selection.

Harrah's collection spanned the entire history of the automobile, including everything from one of the most extensive selections of horseless carriages anywhere right up to the current cars of the day. A stickler for accurate, detailed restoration, Harrah apparently developed his fastidiousness partly in response to an experience with his first collector car. A Maxwell

he bought in 1948 was passed off as being a 1907 model; only later did Harrah discover it was a 1911.

By 1961, Harrah was not just collecting; he was in the car business, opening Modern Classic Motors in Reno, Nevada. A longtime fan of Ferraris, Harrah was not only offered an automobile dealership by Enzo Ferrari, but was also enlisted by Ferrari as the company's West Coast distributor.

With his collection numbering more than 500 cars, Harrah found himself wanting a place to keep the collection and share it with the public. On February 24, 1962, the Harrah's Automobile Collection opened its doors in Reno, by which time it included more than 600 cars. The facility also included a complete restoration shop to service the ever-growing collection and an extensive automotive research library.

After his death, the Holiday Corporation of Holiday Inn fame purchased Harrah's empire, including the car collection—which, by that time, in addition to the more than 1,500 automobiles, included cable cars, buses, and anything else on wheels that had piqued Harrah's interest. In an effort to recoup some of its investment, Holiday promptly announced plans to liquidate the collection.

Casino magnate and car collector William Harrah standing alongside his first collector car, a 1911 Maxwell. Harrah's collection stood at roughly 1,500 autos at the time of his death.

Holiday's plans were greeted with outrage by a diverse group, including collectors, locals, former employees, and even Nevada Governor Robert List, who helped create the National Automobile Museum Foundation. After auctioning off many of the cars, Holiday donated 175 to the Foundation, along with the library. All were moved into a new, 105,000 square-foot (9,755 sq. m) facility in Reno, where the last of William Harrah's collection remains.

Liberace

Above: Liberace was a beloved entertainer with a 40-year career in show business. His cars were part of his act—he used them to make his grand stage entrances.

Right: A sampling of Liberace's collection, as seen at the Liberace Museum in Las Vegas, Nevada. Liberace's were no ordinary cars; each was bejeweled and customized to reflect his flamboyant onstage persona.

The flamboyant pianist Liberace (born Wladziu Valentino Liberace, 1919–87) was an unlikely automotive enthusiast and collector with a unique taste in cars. Liberace's cars were often just as glitzy and over-the-top as he.

Ironically, Liberace had never owned a car until he bought a 1950 Oldsmobile 88 Convertible at age 30. The showman said that the car's name, "88," had attracted him as it also indicated the number of keys on a piano. Liberace did not truly catch the car-collecting fever until one of his television sponsors presented him with a customized 1954 Cadillac El Dorado.

When Liberace moved from television to live performances in the 1960s, he incorporated autos into his act, and lav-ish—and often gaudy—vehicles would chauffer him on and off the stage. These cars included a rhinestone coated 1934 Mercedes Excalibur and a mirror-tiled, pink Volkswagen Beetle customized to look like a Rolls-Royce. The Volkswagen–Rolls was unique in that it was used exclusively to haul one of Liberace's particularly heavy feathered capes on and off the stage.

Another favorite was a gilded Bradley GT kit car based on a Volkswagen Beetle. The gold-flake painted GT resembled a small Mercedes-Benz Gullwing sports car and was upholstered with crushed velour and festooned with a sterling silver candelabrum. Liberace would gush to audiences how fond he was of this car, although he often complained that the little car was particularly hard to get out of.

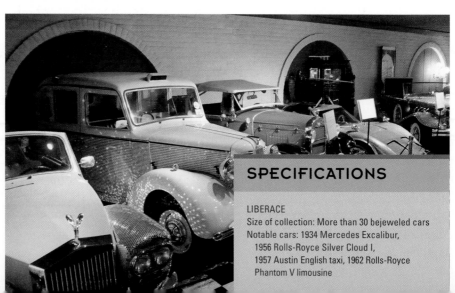

SPECIFICATIONS

LIBERACE
Size of collection: More than 30 bejeweled cars
Notable cars: 1934 Mercedes Excalibur,
 1956 Rolls-Royce Silver Cloud I,
 1957 Austin English taxi, 1962 Rolls-Royce
 Phantom V limousine

"You know that bank I used to cry all the way to? I bought it."

—LIBERACE

CADILLAC RANCH

In 1974, Texan oil heir and art patron Stanley Marsh 3 (b. 1938) commissioned an unusual and soon to be well-known artwork consisting of 10 Cadillacs lined up in a row, their noses buried in the dirt. Cadillac Ranch was born, with models from 1949 to 1963 poised with their tailfins high in the air for all eternity—or at least until the creep of Amarillo development required moving the entire installation two miles farther out of town in the 1990s.

The work was constructed by members of the Ant Farm, a group of renegade architects and artists who used video, performance, and sculpture in their work. Ant Farm members needed a couple of weeks to round up the Cadillacs, including examples from junkyards, used car lots, and private sales. Five days later, with the aid of heavy equipment, the cars were planted, fittingly enough, along old Route 66, now Interstate 40.

The Cadillacs are still there, but almost 35 years of weather and thousands of visitors a year have altered the appearance of the once pretty good looking—and now classic—cars. Depending on your point of view, the dents and graffiti could either be regarded as vandalism or as part of an ever-evolving art project.

Still, perhaps the most recognized of the entertainer's stage cars was a 1954 Rolls-Royce painted in patriotic red, white, and blue for the "Liberace 1976" show during the height of his stage career. The car would bring Liberace onstage in his famous Bicentennial Hot Pants outfit during an elaborate fireworks display while his band played Sousa's "Stars and Stripes Forever." Due to popular demand, Liberace brought back the "Stars and Stripes" Rolls for a Statue of Liberty 100th Anniversary show at New York's Radio City Music Hall in 1986.

Liberace's unique automotive predilections were not limited to the stage—he also owned a refurbished 1957 Austin English taxi that he employed to shuttle friends to and from the Palm Springs airport to his nearby estate. While making the trip, the diesel-powered Austin would tally its passengers' fares in pounds and shillings.

For his own use, Liberace loved to be chauffeured about in a 1962 Rolls-Royce Phantom V limousine. The plush Phantom featured an ornamental wet bar, a telephone, and a rare retractable landau roof. After 68,000 miles of use, Liberace retired the Phantom V from the road and had car customizer John Hancock fit its panels with gleaming, mirrored mosaic tiles. The Phantom then became part of the stage show from the late 1970s through the mid-1980s.

Many of Liberace's more lavish vehicles are now on display at his Las Vegas museum, which the performer created as part of his scholarship foundation.

Despite the ravages of weather and time, the 10 cars of Cadillac Ranch are still visible alongside Interstate 40 in Texas. Writing graffiti on the autos is encouraged, and the cars are repainted from time to time to allow for new decoration.

Harold LeMay

As a young man starting out in business in the 1940s, Harold LeMay (1919–2000) realized that "as long as there are people, there will always be garbage." So LeMay installed a hand-cranked dump box on the back of a 1935 Chevrolet truck and bought himself his first garbage route in Tacoma, Washington.

Obviously, he was right about the garbage and evidently had a good head for business. His company eventually served more than 125,000 customers, and employed about 450 people. Today, LeMay holdings include two refuse companies, a huge recycling concern, an investment firm, and other businesses.

LeMay's success also enabled him to indulge his passion for automobiles. By the time of his death in 2000, LeMay and his wife Nancy had amassed a collection of some 3,000 cars, along with motorcycles, buses, and, of course, a garbage truck or two. All told, it was enough to earn the LeMays a spot in the *Guinness Book of World Records* for the largest privately owned car collection.

> "It seems like it just happened. [Harold] really didn't set out to have this huge collection. He just kept buying cars."
>
> —NANCY LeMAY

SPECIFICATIONS

HAROLD LEMAY
Size of collection: roughly 3,000 cars
Notable cars: 1916 Abadal custom-bodied
  Abadal-Buick, 1930 Duesenberg J convertible,
  1948 Tucker 48 sedan

Unlike more high-profile collectors, LeMay was unflamboyant and to this day many collectors do not know his name. He was not one to frequent upscale car shows like Pebble Beach, and, it is said, he simply bought what he liked. As evidenced by the size of his collection, he liked variety, especially among American cars. The collection that LeMay accumulated is often considered the best representation of the history of American iron ever amassed.

Though he did not find it necessary to rub elbows with the car collecting elite at Pebble Beach, LeMay enjoyed sharing his collection. He and Nancy bought the ideal place to do just that—the 80-acre former Marymount Military Academy in Spanaway, Washington, which became the family homestead. Described by Nancy as being the typical five-bedroom home with a 300-car garage, it might sound like gearhead heaven. For LeMay, with cars parked nose to tail—even in the former gymnasium complete with basketball hoops still in place—it was the bare minimum. Nothing fancy—just enough room for cars, cars, and more cars.

Marymount has also been the setting for the annual Car Show and Open House held every August for more than 25 years. Drawing thousands of visitors, the event was a perfect excuse for LeMay to break out his double-decker buses to shuttle guests around the estate.

Plans are under way for a museum to house the collection and give it a permanent home in Tacoma.

A 1910 Columbia 2-ton flatbed among the LeMay collection, which is lauded for being perhaps the most extensive survey of American automobiles ever accumulated.

Sultan of Brunei

Hassanal Bolkiah, the Sultan of Brunei, has been the leader of his small, Southeast Asian nation since 1967. He is one of the wealthiest men in the world, and has spent lavishly, buying and commissioning rare cars.

The Sultan of Brunei, whose country is sited atop the largest known oil reserves in the world, is one of the world's richest men and is a walking example of what real estate agents mean when they talk about the importance of location, location, location.

His Majesty Sultan Haji Hassanal Bolkiah Mu'izzaddin Waddaulah (b. 1946) is the 29th of his line, which dates back to the fourteenth century. He was also the richest man in the world for some time—though that is no longer the case, he still appears to be quite flush financially.

The sultan has a taste for cars—though maybe a ravenous appetite is a better description. Bolkiah owns some 5,000 vehicles; his collection reportedly includes eight McLaren F1s that sold for $1 million apiece when new; six Dauer 962s—a road-going conversion of a Porsche 962 race car capable of zero to 60 miles (0–96.5 km) per hour in 2.6 seconds; some 350 Rolls-Royces, and too many Mercedes-Benzes to count—including the only right-hand drive CLK-GTR in the world. Designed to compete in the FIA GT championship and powered by a mid-engine V12, CLK-GTRs won all of the titles they competed for in 1997 and 1998.

The sultan also owns many Ferraris, including at least one custom-made

station wagon, a number of Lamborghinis and Porsches, and a lone Lotus. And then there are the motorcycles. The collection is reportedly kept in several warehouses as large as airplane hangars. It is said it can take up to an hour to get a car into the open from its parking spot.

While the sultan obviously likes fast cars, he apparently does not go much for the classics. His taste appears to run primarily to newer, expensive models. And he goes deep. Why have

SPECIFICATIONS

SULTAN OF BRUNEI
Size of collection: roughly 5,000 cars at its peak
Notable cars: McLaren F1, Dauer 962,
   Porsche 962, Ferrari Mythos

The sultan's interest in powerful cars does not end with street models. He has commissioned manufacturers to turn concept show cars into drivable models and also has a collection of retired Formula One race cars. The cars are not exclusively for the sultan's use. He shares the collection with family members, government officials, and other members of the royal household.

one Jaguar XK8 when you can have 25 of them? Perhaps he is just being practical, given Jaguar's reputation for spotty reliability.

The Ferrari Mythos, which existed only as a prototype until the Sultan paid Ferrari to make the car a reality for him. He reportedly owns two of the supercars, which are said to be capable of 180 miles (290 km) per hour.

Nick Mason

Nick Mason (b. 1944), the drummer for legendary rock band Pink Floyd, says his first love was not music but cars. Some of his earliest childhood memories reportedly involve riding with his dad to vintage races in a Bentley that the senior Mason drove competitively at Britain's Silverstone race circuit. Cars have been a big part of his life ever since, including that Bentley. He still has it.

Music, though not his first love, has provided him with the funds to cultivate his car collection, which occupies several hangars and is primarily devoted to racing cars. In addition to his dad's Bentley, Mason owns examples of notable historics from the turn of the twentieth century as well as models as recent as an Enzo Ferrari. Within the hangars, a visitor could also find a Birdcage Maserati, a Type 35 Bugatti, a Jaguar D-Type, and a Ferrari 250 GTO, among others.

The GTO comes with an interesting story. Mason was first taken by the allure of a GTO while watching one race at Goodwood in the early 1960s. Only years later, when the rock-and-roll royalty checks started

SPECIFICATIONS

NICK MASON
Size of collection: 38 cars
Notable cars: Birdcage Maserati, Type 35 Bugatti, 1972 Ferrari 356 GTB/4 Daytona, Model T clown car, Ferrari 250 GTO

rolling in, was he able to realize a childhood dream and purchase a 250 GTO of his own. Going through its logbook after the purchase, he realized his was the very same car he had seen at Goodwood as a boy. A practical man, Mason reports that he has taken his kids to school in it on winter mornings when newer cars would not start. He has said that the GTO is "surprisingly good in the snow."

Other Ferraris in the Mason garages include a 1972 356 GTB/4 Daytona and a 512S that raced at LeMans, only to be seriously damaged by fire while being used in the filming of Steve McQueen's movie *LeMans*. Mason is said to have purchased it for about $12,000 in the 1970s, a fraction of the money later spent to restore it. The several years of finding parts and properly assembling the car are another equation—and expense—entirely.

But not everything in the Mason collection has done hot laps and comes with a racing pedigree. The collection includes a Trabant and a Model T clown car, complete with doors that still fall off on command.

Mason not only believes in driving and even competing in his cars, he contends that they need to work for a living. In fact, the notion of keeping these gems in storage "appalls" him. To that end, all of the cars in his collection are available for hire to makers of films, videos, or for other promotional work.

When not out on a set, the cars are likely to be doing track time because Mason has been driving competitively around the world for more than 40 years—including five stints at LeMans.

Or they might just be under the bright lights being filmed with their doors falling off.

Nick Mason hits the track in his Ferrari 250 GTO. The GTO was a thoroughbred sixties race car, fast, strong, and agile. Mason has affirmed the car's strength by reportedly driving it in the snow when other autos failed to start.

Jay Leno

Comedian and host of NBC's *The Tonight Show*, Jay Leno (b. 1950) regards his car collection a little differently from many others with a fondness for cars. For one, he drives his cars—from his 1906 Baker electric to his 2006 Corvette. Leno is not a guy who goes for roped-off museum pieces.

The cars are impeccably maintained and ready to be shown—however, Leno puts a value on actually using his cars rather than tucking them away in sealed storage. When not being used, the cars reside in the Big Dog Garage, a 17,000-square-foot, purpose-built facility that includes a complete machine shop capable of fabricating parts and body panels for cars that have not had much dealer support for the past hundred years. It also includes a gourmet kitchen, where Leno demonstrates his culinary skills for the benefit of his employees and visitors.

Big Dog is managed by Swiss-born Bernard Juchli, whose family relocated to southern California in the 1960s. Juchli, who owned a Jaguar shop in the Bay Area for years, had been planning to retire when he first met Leno. It seems that Leno's 1948 XK120 broke a camshaft, and everybody said Juchli was the guy to go see. Leno ended up recruiting Juchli to relocate to the Big Dog, where he oversees a small staff, including an engineer who fabricates parts, as well as a paint and bodywork expert.

The common thread in Leno's eclectic mix appears to be that all the cars are fast. Almost

Jay Leno leans up against a 1941 American LaFrance fire truck parked in his Big Dog Garage. Called "the most practical vehicle in Jay's collection," the fire truck bears a signature customization—the water tank was removed to install a tailgate lift used to bring broken-down motorcycles back to the garage.

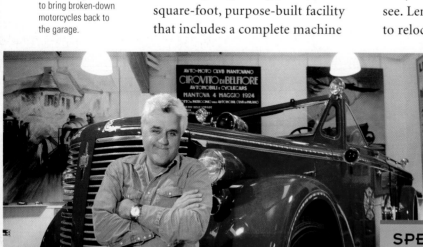

SPECIFICATIONS

JAY LENO
Size of collection: 80 cars, 80 motorcycles
Notable cars: 1906 Baker electric, 1931 Shotwell
    Three-wheeler, 1966 Oldsmobile Toronado,
    1969 Lamborghini Miura

everything in it, according to Leno, is capable of at least 100 mph. Some are capable of far more. Some are simply ridiculous, like the tank car, a custom built, 28-foot-long hot rod powered by a 30-liter, 2,100 pound tank engine plucked from an M-47 Patton tank. The engine's 810 horsepower was not quite enough for Leno, so it is now fitted with twin turbochargers and good for 1,600 horsepower.

Other autos are subtler, like the 1966 Oldsmobile Toronado that looks box stock from the outside, right down to its period red stripe tires. But under the hood is a 1,000-horsepower engine, driving the rear wheels of what rolled out of the factory as a front-wheel-drive car.

Another interesting example is a 1955 Buick Roadmaster, purchased by Leno in 1972 for $350. It is the car that brought Leno to the bright lights of Los Angeles, the car he took his future wife Mavis out for dates in, and the car he drove to his first *Tonight Show* guest appearance. Once Leno's career started to take off, the Buick sat in the shadows for several years until Juchli suggested a bit of a makeover. A cosmetic restoration left it looking completely stock, but things got a little more interesting underneath. A 572 cubic-inch engine pumping out 600 horsepower was

installed, and the original suspension was ditched in favor of a four-wheel independent setup from a Corvette.

The list goes on, and includes a Rolls-Royce powered by a 27-liter V12 from a WWII vintage fighter plane, a couple of classic Duesenbergs, and even a motorcycle powered by a 502 cubic-inch V8. As Leno's fellow Californians and car heads the Beach Boys once said in song, "'Round, 'round, get around, I get around," Leno gets around—and fast.

Leno driving a 1931 Shotwell Three-wheeler, a one-off car designed and built by a Minnesota man who needed a car in his youth, and decided to construct his own. Late in his life, Bob Shotwell decided to donate the car—which is powered by an Indian motorcycle engine—to Leno, because he knew Leno would care for it and keep it intact.

CHAPTER 12

WOMEN AND CARS

ONE HUNDRED YEARS AFTER the introduction of Henry Ford's Model T, which, it is said, put the world on wheels, women remain a distinct minority in virtually all aspects of the car business. Although, according to *Road & Travel* magazine, women purchase an estimated 65 percent of all new cars, more than half of all used cars, and are involved in 95 percent of all automotive purchasing decisions, they currently represent only 7 percent of dealerships' staff in the United States.

In the worlds of automobile manufacturing and racing, women's numbers remain thin, but change is afoot. More and more, carmakers are designing cars with women in mind. Likewise, the women working for auto manufacturers at new car introductions and press events are not only models, but also engineers and executives.

On the racetracks, women drivers have always been a minority and have suffered more than their fair share of slammed doors, lost opportunities, and a general lack of respect from the racing patriarchy. However, the determination, skill, and bravery—both on and off the track—of a handful of female drivers over the years have begun to change the situation. In forms of competition ranging from drag strips, to rallying, to road courses, more women are competing and winning in race cars than ever before.

Here is a look at a few of the women who have worked or are working to change 100 years of automotive culture for the better.

A pioneering race car driver and automotive journalist, Denise McCluggage helped found the magazine *Competition Press*, now known as *AutoWeek*. She was inducted into the Automotive Hall of Fame in 2001, the first journalist to earn such an honor.

Denise McCluggage

Denise McCluggage in the press box. Her long and stellar career in journalism was born of tenacity—as a female writer in the 1950s, she was not allowed in the pits or the press box, but she found ways around these restrictions. She went on to become the first journalist admitted to the Automotive Hall of Fame.

When Denise McCluggage (b. 1927) heard she had been selected as the first automotive journalist to be inducted into the Automotive Hall of Fame, her first response was to ask "Why me?"

Perhaps she was selected because of her long and checkered racing career, or maybe it is because she is an outstanding automotive journalist and photographer who has been at the job for a half-century or so. (McCluggage herself has pointed out that she has been around long enough to remember running boards).

A published author and longtime columnist for *AutoWeek* magazine, McCluggage earned the respect of race drivers partly by being one of them. In the 1950s, she was not allowed in the garage, pits, or press box at the Indianapolis 500 when she was reporting for the *Herald Tribune*. She interviewed drivers through a chain-link fence.

McCluggage figured out other ways to talk to the drivers and get the story, including finding them in hotel lobbies. This, she says, gave her stories that differed from those published elsewhere, making her work stand out.

Upon seeing her first MG TC, the first sports car to land on American shores after World War II, McCluggage announced she had to have one. She later went on to describe the MG as "A loose roller-skate of a car" but that did not keep her from competing both in it and in other MGs.

Like so many racers in the heady days of sports car competition in the late 1940s and '50s, McCluggage drove her car to the track and to work the next day. She graduated from MGs to a Jaguar XK140, eventually scrimping and saving her way to a Ferrari 250 GT—which became both her daily driver and race car. She once stated in *Road & Travel*

"Not always, but sometimes when you're driving one behind another—climbing, descending, dipping, turning—it happens, and you are dancing. The cars are connected. Viscerally, not visibly."

—DENISE McCLUGGAGE

magazine that the Ferrari was her only possession of material value, period, and that she recalls running an entire season on one set of tires.

Her access to the pits and press rooms improved as she racked up laps at Sebring, Daytona, and Germany's Nürburgring, competing against the likes of Stirling Moss, Phil Hill, and Dan Gurney.

Although McCluggage started easing out of the racing scene toward the end of the 1960s, she remains a fixture at automotive events and continues to write a column for *AutoWeek*, a publication that she helped found (originally as *Competition Press*).

Now in her eighties, McCluggage is also still shooting apexes. Ride on, Denise.

Denise McCluggage at speed. Becoming a successful race-car driver enhanced McCluggage's journalistic credibility among the racing patriarchy.

Pat Moss

The younger sister of legendary race driver Stirling Moss may not be as famous as her brother, who had 66 Grand Prix wins under his belt by the time he retired. But Pat Moss (b. 1934) is no slouch, having racked up five European Rally Championships during the 1950s and '60s, along with many individual race victories.

She got her rallying start in 1953, driving a Morris Minor after a stint as navigator for Ken Gregory, her brother's manager. Moving onto

Pat Moss is congratulated by her brother Stirling after finishing first in the 1955 Ladies Handicap race at Goodwood Circuit in England. A groundbreaking female rally driver, Pat Moss won five European championships in her storied career.

SPECIFICATIONS

PAT MOSS
Best finishes:
8th 1960 Netherlands' Tulip Rally
2nd 1960 Coupe des Alpes
1st 1960 Liege-Rome-Liege
1st 1962 Tulip Rally
2nd 1962 East African Safari Rally
3rd 1965 Monte Carlo Classic

"Rallying was like a circus, with groups of Germans and Swedes and French all mingling with each other."

—Pat Moss

faster MGs, Austin-Healeys, and later, Mini Coopers, Moss was regarded as the world's top female rally driver by the early 1960s. She achieved some of her most significant victories driving an Austin Healey.

Sharing wheel duties with codriver Ann Wisdom in 1960, the pair started their season by driving a factory-backed Austin Healey 3000 to a Coupe des Dames—the rallying award given to the highest-placing female team—in the Geneva Rally. They went on to score the first major international victory for Austin Healey's new model by taking first in class and eighth overall in the Netherlands' Tulip Rally. A month later, the two took another class win and finished second overall in the Coupe des Alpes.

They capped their remarkable season in the Healey with a victory in the Liege-Rome-Liege event, often described as the most grueling of all European rallies. Run over some of the most challenging mountain roads of France, Italy, and the former Yugoslavia, the rally covered a brutal 3,300 miles (5,311 km) in 96 hours—with just one hour-long break. To put the significance of this victory in perspective, only 15 of the 83 starters finished this race in 1960. In this race—which has been described as the most difficult rally of all time—the women did not settle for a Coupe des Dames or even a class win; they took first place overall.

By 1961, Moss had moved on to a Mini Cooper—the new high-performance variant of BMC's front-wheel-drive economy car. She immediately helped establish the Mini as a rally car to contend with by winning the 1962 Tulip Rally—in only the car's second outing. From there, the Mini went on to many notable victories until the late 1960s, including an overall win at Monte Carlo.

Moss eventually migrated to Saab, after marrying Swede and fellow rally driver Erik Carlsson (b. 1929), who raced for the Swedish carmaker in the 1950s and '60s. Along the way, he earned the nickname "On the roof," thanks to the position his car sometimes ended up in when competing. Moss, who preferred to keep her wheels under the car, remained competitive after switching to Saab, taking second in the East African Safari Rally in a Saab 96 and a third overall in the 1965 Monte Carlo.

Pat and Erik cowrote a book, *The Art and Technique of Driving*, in 1965. She followed that work with a solo effort about her career, *The Story So Far,* in 1967.

Janet Guthrie

In the overwhelmingly male-dominated world of car racing, Janet Guthrie is truly a pioneer, having been the first woman to compete in both a NASCAR Winston Cup race and the Indianapolis 500. While successful on her own terms, Guthrie also helped pave the way for today's female race car drivers.

Guthrie was born in Iowa in 1938 and raised in Miami, Florida. She earned her pilot's license at age 17 and later became a flight instructor. She earned a degree in physics at the University of Michigan in 1960 and worked as an aerospace engineer for manned-flight projects in the 1960s.

In 1964, she applied for NASA's astronaut program and made it through the first round of eliminations, but did not advance.

Guthrie was taken by the allure of automotive racing. In the mid-1960s, she raced her own cars in many club-racing competitions and later even built her own race cars. By 1972, Guthrie had become a full-time professional race car driver and competed in endurance events, including the 12 Hours of Sebring and the 24 Hours of Daytona. At both races, her teammates were women and they twice won their racing class at Sebring.

Janet Guthrie (number 68) battles the legendary Richard Petty during the World 500 in Charlotte, North Carolina, in 1976.

> "[While racing], your emotional steam, superheated, is harnessed, entirely at the service of your will."
>
> —JANET GUTHRIE

SPECIFICATIONS

JANET GUTHRIE
Best finishes:
12th 1976 NASCAR Winston Cup race, the Charlotte 600
6th 1977 Winston Cup
9th 1978 Indianapolis 500
6th 1979 Milwaukee 200

Janet Guthrie during a press conference in 1978, announcing that Texaco would fund her car and pit crew for her second appearance in the Indianapolis 500. She went on to finish ninth that year.

In 1976, legendary race team owner Rolla Vollstedt invited her to drive one of his team's cars at Indianapolis, but Guthrie failed to qualify for the 500.

Later that year, she competed in her first NASCAR Winston Cup race, the Charlotte 600. She finished 12th despite her car's engine blowing two cylinders with several laps to go. (Louise Smith, who raced in the Winston Cup's precursor, Strictly Stock, was the first woman to compete in NASCAR's top circuit.) Guthrie went on to compete in four more NASCAR races that year and 28 more races in subsequent years, finishing as high as sixth place.

Guthrie became the first woman to earn a starting spot in the Daytona 500 in 1977; later that year she became the first woman to compete in the Indianapolis 500—but engine problems forced her to stop before finishing the race.

Guthrie, who had a hard time getting sponsorships and financial backing for her Indy Car and NASCAR efforts, formed her own Indy team in 1978 and finished an impressive ninth in the Indy 500. In all, Guthrie competed in 11 IndyCar events over the next several seasons and finished as high as sixth at the 1979 Milwaukee 200. Her best Winston Cup finish was also sixth, at Bristol in 1977.

In 2005, Guthrie published her autobiography, *A Life at Full Throttle*. The next year, she was inducted into the International Motorsports Hall of Fame at the Talladega Superspeedway in Alabama. Her helmet and race suit are in the collection of the Smithsonian Institution.

Shirley Muldowney

Early in her drag-racing career, Shirley Muldowney was not taken seriously by many of her male competitors. She eventually became one of the most successful and respected racers in her sport.

Shirley Muldowney (b. 1940) got her first taste of competition driving as a street racer in Schenectady, New York, in the 1950s. In the early 21st century a woman breaking into the world of street racing is unusual; it was virtually unheard of when this upstate New Yorker started ripping it up.

In 1958, the then 18-year-old Shirley made her first run down a real drag strip at New York's Fonda Speedway at the wheel of a 1958 Chevrolet powered by a 348-cubic-inch V8. By 1965, she had earned her National Hot Rod Association dragster license and was married to another former street racer, Jack Muldowney (they divorced in 1972). Her husband built her first real fuel-injected dragster. The pair toured East Coast and Midwest tracks, running match races; she continued to move on to ever-faster cars. By 1969, she was running a monster drag car with two supercharged engines.

Despite winning several trophies, Muldowney still was not taken seriously by much of the racing world, but the naysayers would soon be left in the dust.

Drag racing's Funny Cars, so named because their lightweight and cartoonish body shells bear at least a vague resemblance to street cars, were gaining popularity with fans in the early

SPECIFICATIONS

SHIRLEY MULDOWNEY
Best finishes:
1st 1971 Funny Car Class at the International Hot
   Rod Association's Southern Nationals
1st 1977 NHRA Top-Fuel Championships
1st 1980 NHRA Top-Fuel Championships
1st 1982 NHRA Top-Fuel Championships

'70s. Muldowney and her husband got on the bandwagon, campaigning a pair of Ford Mustangs—*The Bounty Hunter* and *The Bounty Huntress*. She won her first major meet competing in the funny car class at the International Hot Rod Association's Southern Nationals.

However, funny cars turned sour for Muldowney, who suffered through four terrible fires in them before vowing to never compete in a funny car again. The next step was Top Fuel, the crème de la crème of drag racing. Muldowney became the first woman to compete in the category, and the sport's legendary Don Garlits and Conrad "Connie" Kallita signed off on her license to drive the NHRA's fastest cars. She had broken into the top level of the boys' club.

After that, there was no stopping the girl from Schenectady, who became the first woman to break the five-second barrier for the quarter mile and who went on to become the winner of an incredible three NHRA Top Fuel Championships—putting her even with Don Garlits.

The first championship came after Texan Rahn Tobler joined the crew in 1977; he is said to have been a key part of the team's win. Tobler eventually became crew chief and he and Muldowney married 11 years after he joined the team.

Muldowney's ride to the top hit its biggest bump in 1984, when a high-speed crash landed her in a ditch while competing at the Grandnational in Quebec. She did not race again until 1987, and she won her third championship in 1989.

Shirley Muldowney opened doors for other women drivers by first kicking them open herself. In addition to her drag racing career, her honors include being named by the New York State Senate as one of Thirty Women of Distinction, along with Eleanor Roosevelt and Susan B. Anthony. She is also on *Sports Illustrated*'s list of top 100 athletes. She was inducted into the Motorsports Hall of Fame in 1990.

Certainly among the highest honors bestowed on Muldowney was the praise given by competitor Garlits, who has said, "Now, if you ask who do I have the most respect for, I'd say Shirley Muldowney. She went against all odds."

Muldowney retired from racing after the 2003 season.

Shirley Muldowney off to a tire-smoking start while qualifying for the 1974 NHRA Winternationals. She eventually won three NHRA Top Fuel Championships.

Joan Claybrook

Joan Claybrook (b. 1938), who has spent decades at the forefront of efforts to make highways and vehicles safer, got her introduction to politics while growing up in Baltimore in the 1940s. Claybrook's father was a lawyer and city council member who advocated racial integration and helping impoverished citizens with housing and legal services. As a girl, she was pressed into service campaigning for her dad, walking around town with a sandwich board to get the attention of voters.

Attending city council meetings after the election, she watched as one of her father's colleagues slept through a meeting, actually setting an alarm to wake himself up when it was time to go home. The whole experience, she has said, introduced her to the good and the bad of the legislative process at an early age.

After graduating from Baltimore's Goucher College in 1959, Claybrook became one of only a handful of women to rise to a high level position in federal government. After receiving her degree, she worked at the Social Security Administration, preparing reports for President John F. Kennedy's Commission on the Status of Women.

Not until she was working for freshman representative to the U.S. House Jim McKay of Atlanta did she start on the road to becoming a consumer advocate. McKay had read *Unsafe at Any Speed,* Ralph Nader's scathing account of the American car industry's lack of interest in making cars safer and wanted Claybrook to arrange a meeting. She did—that meeting led not only to a lasting friendship between Claybrook and Nader, but also resulted, in 1966, in the first auto safety bill to pass Congress.

The National Traffic and Auto Safety Act required safety belts, padded dashboards, and other basic safety features on all new vehicles. The bill so angered auto industry executives that they hired spies to follow Nader in an effort to find some dirt on him. It also earned Claybrook the nickname "Dragon Lady" with carmakers, who were surprised when they realized that the seemingly harmless, bespectacled woman was investigating the possibility of bringing criminal charges against them. Claybrook took the nickname as a compliment.

In addition to safety equipment in cars, the law created the National Traffic Safety Bureau, which has evolved into the National Highway Traffic Safety Administration (NHTSA). Claybrook went to work for the newly formed agency, but still managed to find time to earn her law degree at Georgetown University by attending classes at night.

"If the auto companies did voluntarily what we paid them to do voluntarily, before the regulatory process takes effect or before there's a lawsuit filed, then we wouldn't have to do our job. But the fact is that they don't."

—JOAN CLAYBROOK

She went on to work for Public Citizen, a consumer advocacy organization formed by Nader in 1971, creating the organization's lobbying arm, Congress Watch, with a mission to promote legislation concerning health, safety, and consumer protection. From 1977 to 1981, Claybrook served as head of NHTSA under President Jimmy Carter, after which she returned to Public Citizen and took over as director. Nader had stepped down in 1980.

Today, Claybrook still serves as president of the organization, which continues to address social and environmental issues.

Joan Claybrook at a 2004 press conference, discussing the reported failures of seat belts in rollover crashes. Claybrook's efforts as a consumer advocate have led to increased American auto-safety standards.

Anne Asensio

As a child, French-born Anne Asensio (b. 1962) dreamed of a career that would somehow involve drawing. The little girl from Versailles, just outside Paris, eventually had a hand in creating the American concept cars—like the Chevrolet Camaro—that wowed auto show attendees in 2006.

Asensio began college pursuing an interest in sculpture, later switching to industrial design. Shortly after her 1986 graduation from the Ecole Nationale Superieure des Arts Appliques et Metiers d'Art in Paris,

Anne Asensio behind the wheel of Saturn's Curve concept car at the 2005 North American International Auto Show. Asensio has won acclaim for her work as an automotive designer in both Europe and America.

Asensio was off to Detroit to further her studies at the prestigious Center for Creative Studies (CCS; now the College for Creative Studies), which boasts that it places more design graduates in the automobile industry than any other school.

By the time she was 24, Asensio was the first and only female designer working at Renault Commercial Vehicles, the truck and van division of the French carmaker. With assistance from Renault, she returned to Detroit for further studies at CCS, during which time Chuck Jordan, who was then head of General Motors design, reportedly offered her a job. She chose to remain with Renault, which rewarded her with a Detroit-based design project.

She returned to France in 1990 to take a new position with Renault's Advanced Design team. There, her concept for a new vehicle won out over eight other

"One of the things I like is thinking forward, thinking really outside the box. I am very happy that in most of my career I was able to work on many products that were very innovative and unconventional."

—ANNE ASENSIO

proposals and led to the wildly successful Megane Scenic of 1997, a sort of mini-minivan that helped usher in a whole new category of people hauler. Later projects at Renault included the Clio subcompact, Twingo minicar, and a concept car called Next, the first Renault design study created entirely by computer.

By 1997, Asensio was chief designer for Renault's small and medium-size vehicles; in that year also, the trade publication *Automotive News* named her Automotive Woman of the Year.

Asensio returned to Detroit in 2000, this time as executive director for General Motors' Brand Character Center, which helps develop the look of all seven of GM's domestic brands. She won accolades from *Automotive News* again that year by being named one of the top 100 women in the automotive industry.

More recognition of her talent came in 2001, when Asensio was featured in a *Fortune* magazine story, "25 Rising Stars," which focused on a next generation of leaders all under the age of 40. *Detroit Business* also added her to their list of Michigan's Most Influential Women that year.

In 2002, Asensio's title at GM expanded to executive director of design, interior design, quality and brand character, and her responsibilities grew to improving interior quality of GM products, along with work on concept vehicles including the Camaro and the Volt.

Asensio left GM in the spring of 2007, presumably to return to France—but not before leaving her mark on the mighty General Motors.

WOMEN MECHANICS

Women often are described as being more practical than men; a good example in the automotive world might be the invention of the windshield wiper. Where most guys who ever slid behind a wheel since the invention of the automobile might have had a tendency to blaze on through the rain even if they could not see, way back in 1903 Mary Anderson (1866–1953) invented a device to clear rain and snow from the recently invented windshield.

Smart woman, that Mary. And not alone among her female peers when it came to innovation: By 1923 more than 175 patents had been issued to women for automotive-related devices ranging from traffic signals to directional signals.

Nevertheless, women have historically been a minority in the auto repair field, though they are now becoming more and more common in car care shops. In the late 1980s, women made up a little over 1 percent of mechanics, but that number has increased to nearly 2 percent within the last two decades.

Milka Duno

The term overachiever comes to mind when talking about Milka Duno (b. 1972). Duno, who now races cars in the United States, got her competitive start as a club racer in her native Venezuela in 1996. Turning pro in 1998, she scored two podium finishes and ended the season fourth overall in the Venezuelan Porsche Supercup Championship that year.

Duno's racing resumé also includes stints in the Ferrari Challenge and Europe's World Series by Nissan. She has competed in both the 24-hour events at Daytona and Le Mans, where she was the only woman of 149 drivers in 2002. Her list of firsts includes being the first woman to win overall a major international sports car race in North America, the first woman to twice win overall a major sports car race in North America, and the first woman to drive the fastest cars in the Rolex Series Daytona Prototypes. Not a bad record for someone who started racing less than 10 years ago.

In addition to her racing career, Duno is a trained naval engineer with

four master's degrees: organizational development, naval architecture, maritime business, and marine biology. She earned three of those degrees simultaneously. Ever the student, Duno has continued her education by attending classes at the Richard Petty Driving School and the Derek Daly Academy Advanced Formula course. If all that is

> "My mentality is you have to work very hard. I appreciate everything God gave me; my role in this moment is to do this. This opportunity, I must take."
>
> —MILKA DUNO

SPECIFICATIONS

MILKA DUNO
Best finishes:
4th 1998 Venezuelan Porsche
   Supercup Championship
1st 2001 Panoz GT Series Championship

not enough to make others look and feel like slackers, she speaks three languages.

In 2000, her track record earned her accolades for "Venezuelan Auto Racing Driver of the Year"; in 2001 she was named "American Le Mans Series 2001 Vice Champion Driver" in the 675LMP class. That year Duno not only won her first race of the year but the Panoz GT Series Championship as well. She advanced to the Barber Dodge Pro Series and competed on ovals all across America. She eventually worked her way up to Grand Am events and the American Le Mans Series Championship, partnering with legendary road racing driver Andy Wallace in a Pontiac. Duno is not finished yet, having recently taken her rookie test for the Indianapolis 500, where she recorded a top speed of 214.13 miles (344.61 km) per hour.

In a male-dominated sport, Duno is dead serious about her career and is pursuing it with the same kind of zeal she applied to earning all those master's degrees.

Grand Am racing is just one of the many forms of racing Milka Duno has participated in. Her Citgo team finished second at the 2007 24 Hours of Daytona, the most illustrious Grand Am race.

Danica Patrick

Danica Patrick has become a racing superstar, and she deserves the attention. Patrick has earned three top-10 finishes at the Indy 500, among other achievements.

Although three women raced in the Indianapolis 500 before her, Danica Patrick (b. 1982) is easily the most recognizable, thanks to her poster-girl looks and wide appeal. Patrick, a spokesperson for various companies, including Honda, Go Daddy Internet Services, and Target department stores, is a familiar face far outside racing circles; she has gained the kind of recognition previously reserved for only a few drivers, Mario Andretti and Richard Petty among them.

Patrick began racing go-karts at age 10, along with her older sister Brooke. Although Brooke eventually grew tired of the sport, Danica persevered and excelled at it, winning many races and several championships. At 16, she dropped out of high school, earned a general equivalency degree, and moved to Canada and eventually England to further her racing career. In England, Patrick raced in entry-level open-wheel race series such as Formula Vauxhall and Formula Ford. In 2000, she placed second in the Formula Ford Festival at the Brands Hatch circuit, the crowning event in the racing series. To date, Patrick's finish in the event is the best by both an American and a woman.

In 2001, Patrick returned to the United States, looking for a ride in open-wheel racing. By 2002, racing legend Bobby Rahal had signed her to a

multiyear racing deal, and Patrick began racing for the team Rahal co-owned with comedian and *Late Show* host David Letterman. Patrick started out in the lower-level Barber Dodge Pro and Toyota Atlantic series. While she showed promise in both series—she took one pole position and finished in the top on the podium in few events—she did not win any races. However, by 2004 the Rahal-Letterman team was sufficiently impressed to allow her to test IndyCars.

To great media hoopla, Patrick made her IndyCar debut the next year. By this time, she was no longer the baby-faced teen of the go-karting circuit; she had blossomed into something of a racing

> "I don't feel like there's anything that I need to do for anybody else. I want to win bad enough for myself anyway, that nothing anybody can say can make me want to win any more."
>
> —DANICA PATRICK

SPECIFICATIONS

DANICA PATRICK
Best finishes:
2nd 2000 Formula Ford Festival
4th 2005 Indianapolis 500
8th 2006 Indianapolis 500
8th 2007 Indianapolis 500

sex symbol, not to mention a driver to be reckoned with. Patrick posted the highest practice speed in 2005, qualifying in fourth position. She led the race for several laps and, despite a few rookie mishaps, she finished fourth—the highest finish ever achieved by a woman at Indy. Later that year, Patrick also won pole positions at the Kansas and Kentucky Speedways.

Patrick's success in the IndyCar series has drawn invective from some drivers and fans. Naysayers have claimed that her relatively low body weight gives her an unfair advantage over her male racing counterparts. Others have charged that her gender and good looks are what earned her a ride with a renowned racing team like Rahal-Letterman. However, nobody in IndyCar racing can refute Patrick's emergence as an ambassador for the sport, as IndyCar racing had languished in the large shadow of NASCAR stock-car racing prior to her arrival on the scene. And her own accomplishments are undeniable. In 2007 she posted her third consecutive top-10 finish at the Indy 500. Critics beware—Danica is here to stay.

Danica Patrick racing in the 2005 Indy 500. She led a total of 19 laps in the race and was in the lead with seven laps to go, but had to stop to refuel. She finished fourth, and earned rookie-of-the-year honors. She has since become a fixture on the IndyCar circuit.

CHAPTER 13

DEVOTED DRIVERS

THERE ARE USED CARS, and then there are well-used cars. Cars today can reasonably be expected to run for at least 100,000 miles, and twice that for most models if they are properly cared for. However, in the 1960s and '70s, most people traded in their personal transportation every two or three years.

While many drivers still turn in their cars every couple of years, now the more likely reason for a trade-in is because the lease is up. A couple of decades ago, however, a driver was lucky if his or her car was still running and had not rusted off the road by the time it was paid for. The general rule was to try not to keep a car for more than 50,000 miles, unless you were looking for trouble. Mechanics, solemnly lowering the hood and wiping off fingerprints with a rag, would gravely advise owners that it was time to let go and move on.

But many march to the beat of their own drum. Irv Gordon, for one, picked up a new Volvo in 1966 and is still driving it a couple of million miles later. In this chapter, we look at record-setting high milers, rally cars, and some conspicuous urban vehicles that rack up miles quickly under tough conditions—New York City taxis.

A taxi streaks past the bright lights of Times Square. For years, yellow-painted Ford Crown Victorias have been the workhorses of New York City, averaging 60,000 miles annually on New York's potholed, cobblestoned, uneven, and congested streets.

Two-Million-Mile Volvo

One day in 1998, retired science teacher Irv Gordon (b. 1942) of Long Island, New York, cruised into the record books while behind the wheel of his 1966 Volvo P1800 coupe. That was the year Gordon was honored by the *Guinness Book of World Records* for reaching "the highest certified mileage driven by the original owner in non-commercial service." At the time, Gordon had managed two million miles of non-commercial motoring in the Volvo he bought new in 1966.

Irv Gordon has been driving his Volvo P1800 for over 40 years. He advocates safe driving as one way to get he longest life out of your car, and urges drivers to pay close attention to the condition of their automobile.

SPECIFICATIONS

1966 VOLVO P1800
Sale price when new: $4,150
Years driven: Over 40
Miles driven: More than 2,500,000

He originally paid a local dealer $4,150 for the P1800, replacing a new car he had just purchased. That one, made by a different manufacturer, broke down on the way home from the dealership, making it a candidate for a somewhat less impressive spot in the

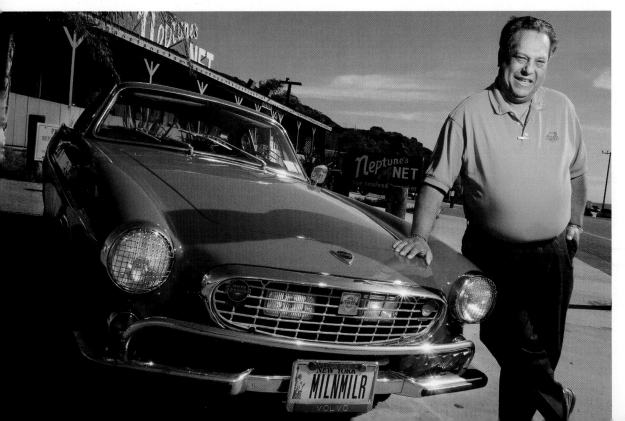

record books. Gordon proceeded to put 1,500 miles on the P1800 during the first 48 hours he owned it. After picking the car up on a Friday, he was back at the dealer Monday for its first service. And Gordon just kept on going.

In addition to a daily round trip commute of 125 miles, Gordon has been known to drive from his Long Island home to, say, Montreal for lunch. This would sometimes confuse lunch dates who did not know him very well and did not understand why he wanted to pick them up first thing in the morning. At least the dates were not expected to drive a leg of the journey—one of Gordon's secrets to making his car last is to never, ever let anybody else drive it.

Gordon says he likes to drive, and one has little reason to doubt him. He needed just five years to put the first quarter million miles on the sporty Volvo, and once he gave up teaching, the miles really began to rack up. He has said that when he got to about 500,000 miles, the car was running better than ever and he knew he had something special.

In addition to those Canadian lunches, he and his Volvo have been all over the United States, and as far away as Mexico. Following the two million mile celebration hosted by Volvo in New York City, Gordon put the P1800 on a boat for a European tour including stops in Holland, Denmark, Germany, and the United Kingdom. The trip also included a pilgrimage to Volvo's world headquarters in Sweden to help celebrate the carmaker's 75th anniversary. Among the supplies packed in the P1800's trunk were four cans of Cheez-Whiz—just in case the local delicacies were not to Gordon's liking.

A stickler for both proper maintenance and safe driving practices, Gordon recommends weekly walk arounds of one's car to inspect directional signals, tires, headlights, and other equipment. He also adheres to a strict schedule of oil changes and other upkeep. He points out that even the most mechanically challenged motorists can check fluids and tire pressure regularly. And—like he did that first day in 1966—he always buckles his safety belt.

As of this writing, Gordon still has his Volvo, which now has a little more than two and a half million miles on the clock. Every time he gets behind the wheel, he breaks another record.

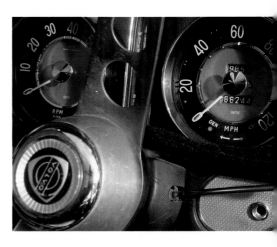

Irv Gordon has long since exceeded the limits of his Volvo's five-digit odometer. At 680,000 miles he had the engine rebuilt, but since then, no major maintenance has been needed, save for a few repairs after accidents.

The Dakar Rally

The rally formerly known as the Paris-Dakar is often regarded as the most challenging car race in the world. In fact, it could really be described as more of an endurance event—or maybe simply an exercise in survival.

Now known simply as the Dakar, the rally embarked from Paris for many years following its 1979 debut. It now begins in Lisbon, Portugal, after officials in the City of Lights lost their enthusiasm for hosting the event. Though many people still call it the Paris-Dakar. Old habits die hard.

Contestants line up in front of the Chateau de Versailles prior to the commencement of the twentieth Paris-Dakar rally in 1997.

SPECIFICATIONS

2006 DAKAR RALLY
Lisbon, Portugal to Nouakchott, Mauritania
Length of rally: 5,619 miles (9,043 km)
Countries crossed: Portugal, Morocco, Mauritania, Mali, Guinea, Senegal
Winners: Luc Alphand/Gilles Picard (car), Marc Coma (motorcycle), Vladimir Chagin/Yakubov/Savostin (truck)

Covering some 7,000 miles over two weeks, the route begins with two days of sand, twisty roads through pine forests, and rocky mountains with treacherous drop-offs.

"A challenge for those who go. A dream for those who stay behind."

—Thierry Sabine, creator of the Dakar Rally

And that is before competitors leave the relatively cushy stages in Portugal and Spain for even tougher motoring in the Sahara Desert.

After leaving Spain, the Dakar begins its trek across the continent of Africa, traveling through some of the harshest conditions imaginable. The route goes through desert terrain in Morocco, Mauritania, Mali, and Senegal, with the lunarlike landscape of the Atlas Mountains thrown in for good measure. Drivers race across high-speed stretches of vast dunes, with next to nothing in terms of landmarks to help them keep their bearings. Less-skilled navigators can be reduced to just picking a set of tire tracks to follow. With any luck, they pick the right ones. When not skimming across dunes, high-speed sections are mixed with slow, technical legs requiring a vehicle that can take punishment, along with skilled driving, a top-notch navigator, and hefty doses of strength and endurance. The longest single-day stage covers more than 500 miles.

The idea for the rally was born in 1977, when founder Thierry Sabine got lost on his motorcycle in the Libyan desert during the Abidjan-Nice rally. After being "rescued from the sands," he returned to France beaten, but determined to share his discovery with as many as possible. Then again, maybe he just wanted others to suffer as he had. He envisioned a route beginning in Europe that would continue to Algiers, eventually ending in Dakar. On December 26, 1978, the first Paris-Dakar competitors rolled out of the Place du Trocadero, and Thierry's dream became a reality.

His vision continues to thrive today; despite the expense, effort, and danger, competitors are eager to sign on. Entries are often turned away months before the start—even though the event is so grueling that almost half of all entrants never cross the finish line.

In addition to cars and motorcycles, the Dakar is open to full-size trucks. In 2007, the roster included 190 cars, 85 trucks, and 264 motorcycles. Of those, 81 of the cars, 16 of the trucks, and 132 of the bikes did not reach the finish, and two motorcyclists lost their lives.

A Kamaz truck rumbles toward the finish line in the final stage of the 2004 Dakar Rally. Kamaz vehicles, which are produced in Russia, have won the truck category of the Dakar Rally seven times.

Mighty Mercedes-Benz

George and Luzstella Koschel took a trip to Germany in 1970, picking up a new Mercedes-Benz 280 SE sedan while there. Purchased through the carmaker's European Delivery program, the Koschels brought the U.S.-spec car back to their California home after touring in Europe.

In a kind of reversal of the European Delivery program, Mercedes paid a visit to the Koschels' 35 years later to see about reacquiring the car for the company's museum in Stuttgart. By that time, the Koschels had managed to put more than one million miles on it—1,019,000 to be exact. A deal was made, and the 280 SE was on its way back to Germany.

Skeptics would rightly point out that in Orange County, California, where the car presumably spent much, if not all, of its life, the mild winter brings little need for corrosive road salt. Also, nobody except the Koschels and Mercedes-Benz seems to know whether the car was on its first engine and transmission or the 11th of each when it was retired.

Still, not many cars reach that kind of milestone, and the Koschels' 280 evidently looked good enough that Mercedes opted to display it at the 2005 Detroit Auto Show before sending it home.

Mercedes has offered owners awards for driving a lot of miles in their cars since the 1960s through the appropriately named High-Mileage Award program. Awards begin at 155,000 miles,

The 1970 Mercedes-Benz 280 SE was known as a durable car, but few drivers got nearly as much longevity out of theirs as George and Luzstella Koschel did. The 1,019,000 miles that the couple drove in their 280 SE sedan was enough to earn the car a place in the collection of the Mercedes-Benz Museum in Stuttgart, Germany.

when according to its Web site, a Star and Laurel badge are awarded; they can be displayed on the Mercedes' radiator grille. A certificate and a presentation folder accompany the badge.

From there, awards go up in increments, although the site indicates nothing about the prize for a cool million miles. One would have to think that the Koschels did not turn over the keys simply for a grille badge and a folder, but a press release made no mention of what the couple received in exchange for their car. It did, however, say they were "considering" a new CLK320 Cabriolet in exchange for packing their car off to the museum.

Although the Koschels' longevity with the 280 is mighty impressive, they do not hold a rearview-mirror-mounted air freshener to a guy with infinite places to go—Gregorios Sachinidis. A Greek taxi driver, Sachinidis holds the known record for excessive Benzing with the 2,852,000 miles he put on his 1976 Mercedes 240D after picking it up used. Sachinidis not only gets the nod

for higher mileage, he did it in six fewer years.

Sachinidis planned ahead: While the taxi was in 24-hour continuous service, he kept three engines around, rotating them through a series of rebuilding, installing, and having a spare.

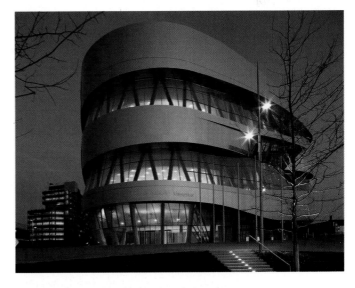

The Mercedes-Benz Museum, in Stuttgart, Germany, opened in 2006. It displays famous automobiles from the legendary automaker's collection, including Gregorios Sachinidis's 1976 Mercedes 240D taxi.

New York City Taxis

A car that travels a million miles at the hands of a caring owner, who keeps it in a garage, adheres to a strict maintenance schedule, and is careful when and where he or she drives it, is one thing. The life of a New York City taxi is another thing entirely. If pampered collector cars are like the show dogs of the automotive world, New York cabs are the working dogs.

New York City has a lot of taxis—many residents do not own cars and use cabs as their primary transportation. In addition to the 13,000 or so medallion cabs with their distinctive yellow paint jobs, another 40,000 or so black sedans and other cars for hire prowl the potholed streets of the city 24 hours a day.

According to the Taxi and Limousine Commission (TLC)—the regulatory agency setting the rules for cabs in the Big Apple—each of the medallion cabs averages 60,000 miles annually, with some traveling as many as 100,000 miles per year pounding the mean streets. And streets are mean to taxicabs.

Many models have been tested for taxi use in the city, but not many can

Ubiquitous yellow cabs in traffic on Park Avenue. New York City taxis are inspected three times per year, and must be retired after three years if they belong to a fleet.

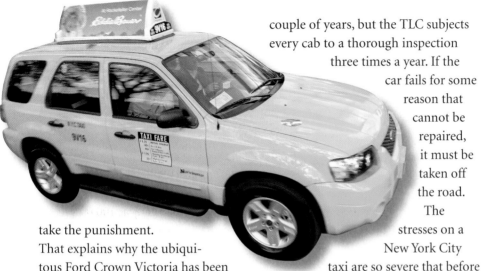

take the punishment. That explains why the ubiquitous Ford Crown Victoria has been top of the heap of the heaps for hire for years. Although its antiquated design dates back to a platform first seen on the road in the 1970s, the Crown Vic—with its trucklike body and on-frame design—has proved tough enough for taxi duty. An added appeal for owners is that Ford, having paid for the tooling years ago, offers the cars and replacement parts relatively cheaply.

New York City rules require that medallion cabs be purpose-built new cars when first put into service and must be retired after three years if part of a fleet—by which time they may have more than a quarter of a million hard miles on them. Owner-operated cars can stay on the road for two more years, based on the assumption that owners take better care of their cars. Hybrid models are allowed another couple of years, but the TLC subjects every cab to a thorough inspection three times a year. If the car fails for some reason that cannot be repaired, it must be taken off the road. The stresses on a New York City taxi are so severe that before the TLC considers a new model for widespread use, a sampling of two or three must be put into service for a year—the jury is out until the cab comes back in. That, combined with a set of specifications detailing everything from minimum legroom to maximum horsepower further limits the number of models available for taxi duty.

The part most often replaced is the rear passenger door, which, on average, is opened and closed 90 times a day. If that does not sound like a lot, go out and give it a try. Then, do it again tomorrow, and the next day, and as long as you can stand it or until the door falls off. Then—if you still have the strength—hail a cab to go where you need to go. Chances are you will not have the energy left to drive.

The Ford Escape hybrid is the probable future of the New York City taxi. As an SUV, the Escape should prove sturdy enough to weather the abuse of city streets, and as a hybrid, it will meet New York mayor Mike Bloomberg's pledge to field a full fleet of hybrid cabs by 2012.

Glossary

AERODYNAMIC DRAG. The resistance caused by a car as it moves and displaces the air in its path. The drag a car creates is measured as the "coefficient of drag." Typically, vehicles that are more boxy displace more air and create more resistance while moving than those with sleeker bodies and therefore have a greater coefficient of drag.

ALL-WHEEL DRIVE. An automotive drive system that provides power to all four wheels for extra traction in all driving conditions. Most provide power to all four wheels at all times, but some systems only engage all four wheels when additional grip is needed. Unlike four-wheel drive, all-wheel drive does not offer low-range gearing for driving off-road.

ANTILOCK BRAKING SYSTEM. Also known as ABS, antilock braking modulates and reduces brake pressure in individual wheels. This helps keep a car from going into a skid and allows the driver to better maintain control of a vehicle during an emergency stop.

BIOFUEL. Any fuel that is derived from organic matter, like plants and even animal waste. Biofuels can be solid, liquid or gas. Common biofuels used in cars include ethanol and biodiesel.

BOXER. An engine where all the cylinders are arranged horizontally. Boxer engines can have different numbers of cylinders, although the most common have four or six. Boxers are relatively more compact than V-shaped and inline engines. Boxer engines are often found in Subaru, Porsche, and Volkswagen models. Boxers come by their name because the engine's pistons resemble a boxer striking together his fists at the beginning of a bout.

CARBON FIBER. Very thin, flexible, and brawny strands of carbon that are often integrated with plastic or other polymer resins to create strong, but extremely light automotive parts such as body panels.

CLUTCH. A device that engages and disengages two working parts in a vehicle's drivetrain and allows for the smooth changing between the transmission's gears. It is also the word used for the pedal that often operates the clutch in a car with a manual transmission.

COMPOSITE. A blend of non-metal materials used in certain car parts that substitute for steel and aluminum components. Composites typically contain combinations of plastics and carbons and are lighter and stronger than steel, but much more expensive.

COUPE. A two-door four-seat vehicle characterized by a sleek design and usually minimal backseat and cargo space.

CYLINDER. The chamber inside which a piston moves. Cylinders are arranged in an engine block, which is cast from either iron or aluminum.

DRIVESHAFT. The mechanical component that transfers power from the engine and transmission to the wheels.

DRIVETRAIN. All the components in a car that send power to the drive wheels. This includes the car's engine, transmission, and the rotating shafts extending to the wheels. On electric-hybrid cars, the drivetrain includes the car's electric motor.

ETHANOL. A biofuel created from organic products, typically corn in the United States and sugar cane in Brazil. Cellulosic ethanol, a newer form of ethanol, can come from many different organic products, such as switchgrass and wood byproducts.

FORMULA ONE. An open-wheel race series that is very popular in Europe, Asia, and South America, but only mildly popular in the United States. The cars are similar in shape and size to American IndyCars, but are typically driven on complex road courses, instead of ovals.

FOUR-WHEEL DRIVE. Also known as 4WD and 4x4, four-wheel drive is a drivetrain system that allows all four wheels to receive power from the engine. Four-wheel drive can be full-time, meaning that all wheels always receive power, or part-time, meaning the driver must select whether two or four wheels drive the vehicle. Unlike all-wheel drive systems, four-wheel drive has low-range gearing for use in off-road or harsh or hazardous conditions such as traveling across rocks, snow, or sand.

GEARBOX. Typically used as an alternative name for a transmission, a gearbox is actually just the system of gears that transmits power from the engine to the driveshaft.

HORSEPOWER. A common unit of measurement used to determine an engine's power. Because a unit of "horsepower" has many definitions, it is widely being replaced internationally by the standard measurement for power, the Watt. However, the term remains popular in the United States. Automotive engineers define it as the strength needed to lift 550 pounds one foot off the ground in one second or to lift one pound 550 feet up in the air, in the same amount of time.

HYBRID. Also known as a gas-electric hybrid, a car that is powered by both direct-current battery power and by ignited gasoline. Hybrids rely on electronics to determine what fuel or combination of fuel is best suited to current driving conditions.

HYDRAULIC. Any mechanical system in an automobile that relies on the pressurized displacement of fluids. Modern braking and steering systems are most often hydraulic.

INDYCAR. A general term used to describe cars that compete at the Indianapolis 500 race, the premier open-wheel race in the United States. IndyCar is also a term used to describe two racing series whose penultimate race is the 500—the IndyCar World Series, in the 1980s and '90s, and the current IndyCar Series, sanctioned by the Indy Racing League.

INLINE ENGINE. An engine where all of the cylinders are aligned in a single row. Inline engines are usually found in four-cylinder configurations, but five- and six-cylinder inline engines are not uncommon. In the 1930s, before the advent of the V8, the "straight-eight" inline engine was considered a superior automotive engine.

KIT CAR. An automobile that is assembled by the buyer who purchases a kit that contains plans and parts. Some kit cars are converted from an existing automotive platform. The Volkswagen Beetle was a popular car for kit conversions.

MONOCOQUE. A building technique that supports a structural load using an object's external skin, rather than from an underlying framework. Like unibody construction, which is similar technique, monocoque construction helps keep a car's weight low. Monocoque construction is common in both aircraft and automotive construction.

NASCAR. An acronym for National Association for Stock Car Auto Racing, NASCAR is a motorsports sanctioning body that supports three automotive racing series, The Nextel Cup (formerly the Winston Cup), the Busch Series, and the Craftsman Truck Series. Often, NASCAR is used just to refer to the Winston Cup, which is by far the largest of the three series.

PILLAR. The columns on a car that support the roof. They are commonly labeled alphabetically from front to back. For example, the pillar at the front of the car's cabin is known as the A-pillar.

SCCA. The acronym for Sports Car Club of America, the SCCA is the sanctioning body for many amateur, semiprofessional, and professional motorsports events including road race, rally, and autocross events.

SEDAN. A four-door fixed-roof car and sometimes a larger two-door car that has plenty of rear seat room.

SPYDER OR SPIDER. A two-seat convertible sports car, often of European manufacture.

STOCK. An automobile, or its components, as they are generally available to the public. If a car comes with many specialized and unique performance or luxury components, it is generally known as a customized, not a stock vehicle. Stock car racing got its name because the cars used in the early days were derived from the stock models that could be bought from a manufacturer. Ironically, there is nothing "stock" about today's highly sophisticated NASCAR stock cars.

SUPERCHARGER. A mechanically driven compressor that is used to force additional air into an engine's combustion chamber. Superchargers are similar to turbochargers, but do not use the force from exhaust gases to generate compressed air.

THROTTLE. The device that regulates the flow of fuel to the engine. It is typically controlled by the throttle pedal, which is often known as the "gas pedal." An engine's power can be increased or decreased by applying or removing pressure to the throttle pedal.

TORQUE. The force needed to cause change in rotational motion. Torque is typically measured in pound-feet.

TRACTION CONTROL. An automotive system that detects if a wheel is losing grip. If so, the system applies braking and may reduce engine power to minimize this loss of grip.

TRANSMISSION. A system of gears that transmits mechanical power from an engine or electric motor to a rotary output device such as a car's driveshaft. Transmissions also provide a reverse gear to allow the car to move backwards. Today, most cars come with automatic transmissions, where the vehicle selects the gear. Manual transmissions, where the driver selects the gear, are becoming more rare. However, many automatic transmissions now provide clutchless manual overrides.

TURBOCHARGER. A device that provides more power to an engine by using energy from a car's exhaust to force compressed air into the engine's combustion chambers, which in turn improves engine performance.

UNIBODY. An automotive construction technique that uses the car's body panels to create structural rigidity rather than an internal framework. Unibody construction saves weight and typically provides better handling and ride than vehicles constructed on an internal framework.

V6. A six-cylinder engine with cylinders arranged in two groups of three and forming a V shape. The V6 is the second most common type of engine after the inline four-cylinder. The V6 was introduced in the early 1950s on the European models such as the Lancia Aurelia. GMC and Buick later introduced V6's in the United States as lighter and smaller alternatives to V8 engines. Today, V6s are well suited to both front- and rear-drive configurations and often provide a lot of power for their relatively compact size.

V8. A V shaped engine with eight cylinders in two groups of arranged in perpendicular angles (typically 90 degrees) from each other. V8s are common in automobiles and small aircraft and are notable for the high amount of horsepower and torque that they produce compared to four-cylinder or V6 engines.

WAGON. A vehicle that provides an extended rear cargo area with a door, rather than a trunk, for easy cargo access. Sport-utility vehicles are sometimes also called wagons because they use a similar vehicle layout.

Find Out More

BOOKS

Adler, Dennis. *The Art of the Automobile: The 100 Greatest Cars.* HarperCollins, 2000.

Cheetham, Craig. *Supercars: The World's Most Exotic Sports Cars.* Motorbooks, 2006.

Cheetham, Craig. *The Encyclopedia of Classic Cars.* Thunder Bay Press, 2003.

Doyle, David. *Standard Catalog of U.S. Military Vehicles.* Krause Publications, 2003.

Jackson, Kevin. *Discover the Hovercraft.* Flexitech, 2004.

Lazarus, William P. *The Sands of Time: A Century of Racing in Daytona Beach.* Sports Publishing, 2004.

Moity, Christian. *24 Hours of Le Mans 2004 (Endurance Is Le Mans).* Chronosports Editeur, 2005.

Mueller, Mike. *Motor City Muscle: High-Powered History of the American Muscle Car.* Motorbooks, 1997.

Olsen, Russ. *Route 66 Lost and Found: Ruins and Relics Revisited.* Voyageur Press, 2006.

Pace, Harold. *Vintage American Road Racing Cars, 1950-1970.* Motorbooks, 2004.

Wyss, Wallace. *Shelby: The Man, The Cars, The Legend.* Motorbooks, 2007.

Young, Anthony H. *Lunar and Planetary Rovers: The Wheels of Apollo and the Quest for Mars.* Springer Praxis Books, 2006.

WEBSITES

Amphibious cars
http://www.amphicar.com

Bill Harrah
http://www.harrahs.com/harrahs-corporate/media-company-history.html

Bugatti Veyron
http://www.bugatti-cars.de/bugatti/index.html

Cadillac Ranch
http://currents.ucsc.edu/03-04/01-19/ant_farm.html

Corvette Z06
http://www.chevrolet.com/corvette

Dakar Rally
http://www.dakar.com

Ferrari
http://www.ferrariusa.com

Greasecars
http://biodiesel.infopop.cc

Harold LeMay
http://www.lemaymuseum.org/

Honda FCX
http://world.honda.com/FuelCell/

Indianapolis Motor Speedway history
http://www.indianapolismotorspeed-
way.com/history

Koenigsegg
http://www.koenigsegg.com

Lamborghini
http://www.lamborghini.com

Lunar Rovers
http://starchild.gsfc.nasa.gov/docs/
StarChild/space_level2/apollo15_
rover.html

Mars Rovers
http://marsrovers.nasa.gov/home

McLaren F1
http://www.mclarenautomotive.com

Mercedes Gullwing
http://www.mercedes-benz.com/
content/mbcom/international/
international_website/en/com/
Brandworld_Museum.html

Model T Ford
http://www.hfmgv.org

Oscar Meyer Weinermobile
http://www.kraftfoods.com/om/
omm_wienermobile.htm

Porsche
www.porsche.com

Saleen
http://www.saleen.com

Smithsonian Institution America on
the Move
http://www.americanhistory.si.edu/
onthemove

Stanley Steamer
http://www.stanleymuseum.org

STP Turbine car
http://www.stp-uk.com/extra41.html

Tesla Roadster
http://www.teslamotors.com/index.
php

Zippo car
http://www.zippoclick.com/zippocar

At the Smithsonian

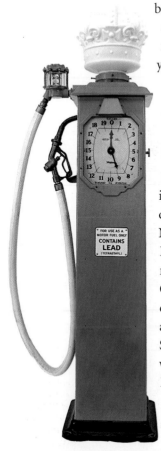

Although British scientist James Smithson had never traveled to the United States, he stipulated in his will that should the nephew he designated as his beneficiary die without heirs, his estate would go to the creation of an institution, bearing his name, in Washington, D.C. Smithson's vision of "an establishment for the increase and diffusion of knowledge among men" began to take shape shortly after the death of the childless nephew in 1835. After several years of sometimes-heated debate, an Act of Congress established the Smithsonian Institution as a trust in 1846.

Today, the Smithsonian is the largest museum complex and research organization in the world, comprising 16 distinct museums and the National Zoo, in Washington, D.C. Two more Smithsonian museums exist in New York City. The National Museum of African American History and Culture will become the Smithsonian's 19th museum when it opens on the National Mall a decade from now.

The Smithsonian's collection of horseless carriages and automobiles is extensive. The oldest model in the collection is a Dudgeon steam wagon dating from 1866. Newer models, such as a 1986 Dodge Caravan and a 1997 General Motors EV1 electric car, are represented as well. The collection, which began with a Balzer automobile donated by inventor Stephen M. Balzer in 1899, now contains more than 60 unique cars. Normally, no more than 12 to 15 are on display at any given time, with the rest either in storage or on loan to other museums. A wide variety of automobiles is represented in an effort to provide an accurate history of cars as part of American culture. The collection includes everything from racing and experimental cars to station wagons to a well-customized Ford LTD lowrider.

America on the Move, at the National Museum of American History, is the Smithsonian's most recent automotive-related exhibit, chronicling how transportation transformed American culture and forever changed the national landscape. The exhibit follows the history of the automobile from its invention to the present day, documenting the sweeping changes both instigated and adapted to by the car. It shows how America developed into a nation of drivers—especially once cars became less expensive, more reliable, and not just playthings for the wealthiest Americans.

The exhibit includes a Model T Ford—the first automobile produced on a moving assembly line—which probably did more to change America to a driving nation than any other model. During the Model T's nearly 20-year production run—from 1908 to 1927—cars became a common sight outside middle-class houses, and people began to live farther and farther from their jobs.

The exhibit also includes a 1903 Winton—the first car ever to complete a cross-country road trip, thus kicking off a century-old tradition. It is displayed stuck in a gully—a position that

This 1894 Balzer automobile was the first car acquired by the Smithsonian. It was described, at the time, as an "experimental 4 wheeled road carriage, driven by rotating gasoline engine."

The General Motors EV1 was a groundbreaking electric car developed by GM and leased to consumers. In 2003, General Motors decided that the car was not commercially viable, and discontinued the project, after recalling all EV1s in existence. However, one was donated to the Smithsonian.

travelers H. Nelson Jackson and Sewall Crocker found themselves in more than once on their trip. The display also includes much of the gear the men would have needed for their voyage, including a block and tackle to help get the Winton unstuck.

Visitors to the exhibit can follow the development of our mobile culture right through the birth of suburbia and the evolution of the nation's highway

system. Photographs and artifacts chronicle Depression-era travelers heading west in hopes of finding a better life and the development of the family-camping craze that followed in more prosperous times.

In addition to a wide assortment of vehicles, including pickup trucks, sedans, convertibles, station wagons, a bus, and even a 1984 Peterbilt 359 over-the-road tractor, you can see examples

of early parking meters, traffic signals, gas pumps, period tools, and other memorabilia.

At the Smithsonian's Air and Space Museum, visitors can get an up-close look at a Lunar Roving Vehicle like the LRVs used by astronauts in the Apollo space program. The display model is one of eight built as test units by Boeing before the three used on missions were built.

A visit to the Smithsonian Institution is a worthwhile trip for anyone interested in the history of the United States. The automobiles and exhibits on display at the National Museum of American History will captivate car buffs, but even those who are not interested specifically in transportation will enjoy learning how the automobile has shaped American culture and vice versa. When you go, allow plenty of time and wear good walking shoes. It will be worth it.

Left: This Lunar Rover, a test vehicle used by NASA, is on display at the National Air and Space Museum.

Below: The National Museum of American History houses the Smithsonian car collection. The museum is on the National Mall, and is currently undergoing a renovation. It will reopen in the summer of 2008.

Index

Acknowledgments and Credits

Cliff Weathers helped shape this book, contributed ideas and his infectious enthusiasm, and wrote many of the spreads. Without his expertise, particularly in military and green cars, a big project would have been bigger.

Kristin Park Travers is my life partner, wife, first reader, and reality check. She and friends Jamie Kitman and Chris Pfouts believed I was a writer long before I did.

Rik Paul, Eric Evarts, Jeff Bartlett, and Jon Linkov, all fellow gear heads and colleagues at my day job, contributed ideas and encouragement.

Thanks also to Eddie Alterman, Marcel Brousseau, Michael Cunningham, John Hagman, Dan Johnston, Dave Kinney, Joe Lorio, Ariane Orenstein, Bo Orloff, Joe Ranker, Barry Spyker, and Pat Yeaters.

This book is dedicated to two extremely talented and inspirational women: Helen Floyd Travers and Joni Zaccara Park.

The author and publisher also offer thanks to those closely involved in the creation of this volume: Peter Liebhold and Roger White of the Division of Work and Industry at the National Museum of American History; Ellen Nanney, Senior Brand Manager, Katie Mann, and Carolyn Gleason with Smithsonian Business Ventures; editor Christina Wiginton of Smithsonian Books; Collins Reference executive editor Donna Sanzone, editor Lisa Hacken, and editorial assistant Stephanie Meyers; consultant Tracy Powell of *Automotive Quarterly* and Powell House Publishing and Communications; Hydra Publishing president Sean Moore, publishing director Karen Prince, editor Marcel Brousseau, senior editor/designer Lisa Purcell, editorial director Aaron Murray, art director Brian MacMullen, designers Erika Lubowicki and Ken "Hollywood" Crossland, production editor Eunho Lee, picture researcher Ben DeWalt, copyeditor Carole Campbell, copyeditor Suzanne Lander, editors Rachael Lanicci, and Andy Lawler, proofreader Ward Calhoun, indexer Amber Rose, and interns Gabrielle Kappes and Matt Gross. Additional thanks to Norbert Vance, Helga Pollock, Andrew S. Hartwell, Charles Phoenix, Charles L. Gilchrist, Thomas Strankowski, Matt Gray, Clarence Reed, Randy Lloyd, Edwin van Nes, Carl Madson, Warren Jones, Tom Burnside, Terry Lobzun of RM Auctions, Inc., Jennifer Schmitt of Barrett-Jackson Auction Co., Holly Wood of the LeMay Museum, Denise Sins of the National Automobile Museum (the Harrah Collection), Tom Bonsall of TK Automobilia, Zoë Schafer of LAT Photographic, and everyone at the GM Futurliner Restoration Project.

CREDITS

The following abbreviations are used: PR—Photo Researchers, Inc; SS—ShutterStock; LoC/PP—Library of Congress, Prints and Photographs Reading Room; AP—Associated Press; NMAH—National Museum of America History; SI—Smithsonian Institution

(t=top; b=bottom; l=left; r=right; c=center; bg=background)

From the Model T to the Moon
iii © Automobili Lamborghini Holding S.p.A **ivbg** LoC/PP **vi** SS/Tomasz Pietryszek **1** AP **2t** AP/MF **2b** SS/Max Earey **3** AP/Chris Young-PA **4** LoC/PP **5** SS/Max Earey **6** AP **7** AP

Chapter 1: Supercars
8bg *Division of Work and Industry*, NMAH/SI /© DaimlerChrysler LLC **10bg** © 2002 Bugatti Automobiles S.A.S **10tl** SS/ oksanaperkins **12** Wikimedia **13tl** photo © Adam Lawrence-Slater **13br** Wikimedia **14** © Automobili Lamborghini Holding S.p.A **15tl** Wikimedia **15b** © Automobili Lamborghini Holding S.p.A **16** Image © Carl Madson Photography **17t** © 2005 Ruben Arakelyan, www.rubenarakelyan.com **17b** photo © Tyrone Milner **18tl** Wikimedia **18b** Wikimedia **19** AP/Jean-Claude Ernst **19bg** SS/ afaizal **20cl** Wikimedia **20br** © 2001 Porsche Cars North America **21tl** © 2001 Porsche

Cars North America **21cr** Photo © John Dewsnap **22** Copyright Koenigsegg Automotive AB 1994-2004 **23tr** Copyright Koenigsegg Automotive AB 1994-2004, Photo by James Holm **23bl** Copyright Koenigsegg Automotive AB 1994-2004, Photo by Thorvaldur Örn Kristmundsson **24** AP/Bugatti **25tr** Wikimedia **25br** Photo by Mike Helde **25bg** © 2002 Bugatti Automobiles S.A.S **26** © 2007 General Motors and Wieck Media Services, Inc. **27tr** Wikimedia **27br** © 2007 General Motors and Wieck Media Services, Inc.

Chapter 2: Extreme Race Cars
28 State Library and Archives of Florida **30** State Library and Archives of Florida **31** LoC/PP **31bg** State Library and Archives of Florida **32** AP **33** AP **35** Photo © Charles L. Gilchrist, www.gilchristbnw.com **36b** Wikimedia/Morven **36br** Wikimedia/Morven **36bg** Wikimedia **37** © RM Auctions, Inc. **38** Andrew S. Hartwell/ashautomobilia.com **39** Andrew S. Hartwell/ashautomobilia.com **40** LAT Photographic **41tr** AP/Anastasi **41** edvvc from Flickr.com

Chapter 3: Otherworldly Cars
42 NASA/Harrison H. Schmitt **44** AP/Bill Reinke **45** AP/Chris Young **46** AP **46bg** Wikimedia/Andrew Berridge **47tr** ©iStockphoto.com/Tom Dautlich **47br** PR/Skyscan **48** © 2007 Warren Jones, www.snow-trac.com **49tr** © 2007 Warren Jones, www.snow-trac.com **49bl** photo by Kevin O'Donnell **50tr** AP/Donna McWilliam **50b** Wikimedia/© Moller International, USA **51** SS/aaron kohr **52** Wikimedia/NASA **53** Wikimedia/NASA **54** NASA/JPL/Cornell University/Maas Digital **55tl** NASA **55br** PR/NASA

Chapter 4: Cars and Marketing
56 photo © Matt Gray, mattgrayphotography.com **58bg** Wikimedia/Ryan Durham **58** AP/Carlos Osorio **59** Charles Phoenix Collection **61** photo © Nathan Bittinger **62** © Barrett-Jackson Auction Co. 2007 **63** Photo by Jonathan Eziquiel-Shriro **64** © Barrett-Jackson Auction Co. 2007 **65** AP **66** Norbert Vance, Eastern Michigan University **67** AP/RM Auctions

Chapter 5: Groundbreaking Automobiles
68bg Division of Work and Industry, NMAH/SI [#2003-32651] **68tl** Wikimedia/DeFacto **70bg** Division of Work and Industry, NMAH/SI [#2003-32655] **70** Division of Work and Industry, NMAH/SI **71** Wikimedia/Infrogmation **72** U.S. Patent Office **73** photo © Clarence Reed **74** © RM Auctions, Inc. **75tl** U.S. Patent Office **75cl** U.S. Patent Office **75br** © RM Auctions, Inc. **76** Wikimedia/Arcturus **77tr** Wikimedia/Frode Inge Helland **77bg** Wikimedia/Ton1/citroen **78** photo © Brian T. Meacham **79** Wikimedia/ Sfoskett **80** Wikimedia/Rama **81tl** U.S. Patent Office **81br** Wikimedia/Rama **82bg** Division of Work and Industry, NMAH/SI /© DaimlerChrysler LLC **82** photo © Randy Lloyd **83** Photo © Randy Lloyd **84bg** SS/ronfromyork **84** SS/Hashim Pudiyapura **85** Wikimedia/ Lothar Spurzem **86** Wikimedia/DeFacto **87tr** Wikimedia/DeFacto **87br** © The British Motor Industry Heritage Trust **88t** AP/J. Duricka **88b** Wikimedia/Bull-Doser **89** Wikimedia/Bull-Doser

Chapter 6: Military Vehicles
90bg AP/Joe Rosenthal **90tl** Wikimedia/ John A. Lee, USMC **92** Division of Work and Industry, NMAH/SI [#38-171] **93** Wikimedia **94tr** Photo by James Tworow, vehicle owned by the Reynolds Alberta Museum, Wetaskiwin, Alberta, Canada **94bl** Photo by Elizabeth Watson **95** LoC/PP **96** AP/Peter De Jong **97** Wikimedia/ Michi1308 **98** AP **99** TKAutomobilia.com

Chapter 7: Green Cars
100 AP/Honda Motor Co. **102** Division of Work and Industry, NMAH/SI [#77-1187] **103t** Division of Work and Industry, NMAH/SI [#MAH-30987] **103br** Division of Work and Industry, NMAH/SI [#MAH-38419] **104** AP/Charles Warner **105tr** AP/Kevin Goldy **105bl** AP/Denis Poroy **106** Division of Work and Industry, NMAH/SI [#2005-5757] **107** Division of Work and Industry, NMAH/SI [#2005-5767] **108** AP/Kiichiro Sato **109** AP/Kiichiro Sato **111t** Photo by Andrew Carabino **111b** AP/Toyota **112** Wikimedia/fogcat5 **113** Wikimedia/fogcat5

114 AP/Honda Motor Co. **115tl** AP/Honda Motor Co. **115cr** Wikimedia/ (flickr/machu)

Chapter 8: Lemons and Critical Flops
116 AP **118** Wikimedia/Christer Johansson **119** AP **120** Wikimedia/Zouf **121** Wikimedia/Sfoskett **122** Wikimedia/Morven **123** Wikimedia/IFCAR **124** Wikimedia/burts **125** Wikimedia/Asterion **126** AP **127tl** Photo by Caine Langford **127bl** Photo by Caine Langford **128** AP **129tl** AP/jch **130** Photo by Mike Baehr **131** Photo by Mike Baehr **132** © 2007 General Motors and Wieck Media Services, Inc. **133** © 2007 General Motors and Wieck Media Services, Inc. **133** © 2007 General Motors and Wieck Media Services, Inc.

Chapter 9: Money is no Object
134 Photo © Thomas Strankowski **136** Photo by David van Mill **137bl** Photo by David van Mill **137br** Photo by David van Mill **138bl** Wikimedia **138tr** Wikimedia/ Chris J. Moffett **139** Courtesy of the GM Futurliner Restoration Project, www.futurliner.com. Bus owned by the National Automobile and Truck Museum of the United States **140** AP/HO **141tl** Wikimedia/Ignis **141br** Wikimedia/Ignis **142** Photo © Thomas Strankowski **143b** Wikimedia/ Jagvar **144** Photo © Geoff Foley **145** Photo © Geoff Foley **146bl** Wikimedia/Späth Chr **146tr** Wikimedia/Jagvar **147** SS/Yan Vugenfirer

Chapter 10: Cars of the Rich and the Infamous
148bg SS/ Todd Taulman **150bg** AP/Richard Sheinwald **150tl** AP/U.S. Coast Guard, Fireman Gregory Wald **152** Wikimedia **153** AP/Paul Sancya **154** AP/U.S. Coast Guard, Fireman Gregory Wald **155** AP/Cristobal Herrera **156** AP/Martin Meissner **157** © RM Auctions, Inc. **158** San Antonio Express-News/ Kin Man Hui **158tr** AP/Waco Tribune Herald **159br** AP

Chapter 11: Collectors and their Collections
160 AP/Marty Lederhandler **162t** © Barrett-Jackson Auction Co. 2007 **162b** © Barrett-Jackson Auction Co. 2007 **163** AP **164bl** Photo courtesy of the National Automobile Museum (The Harrah Collection), Reno, Nevada **164br** Photo courtesy of the National Automobile Museum (The Harrah Collection), Reno, Nevada **165** Photo courtesy of the National Automobile Museum (The Harrah Collection), Reno, Nevada **166tl** AP **166b** photo © Paul Steven Lawrence **167** photo © The one and only Superherochika, Erika Lubowicki **168t** LeMay Museum **168b** LeMay Museum **169** LeMay Museum **169** AP **170tr** AP/Haji Hassanal Bolkiah **171** Image by Edwin van Nes **172** AP/Christophe Ena **173** LAT Photographic **174** AP/Chris Pizzello **175** NBC Photo

Chapter 12: Women and Cars
176 Tom Burnside Motorsport Archive **178** Tom Burnside Motorsport Archive **179** Tom Burnside Motorsport Archive **180** LAT Photographic **182** AP/Harold Valentine **183** AP/Marty Lederhandler **184** AP/George Brich **187** AP/Evan Vucci **188** © General Motors/Joe Polimeni **189** AP/Waterloo Courier, Sarah Schutt **190** AP/Matt York **191** AP/Matt York **192tl** AP/Tom Strattman **193** AP/Darron Cummings

Chapter 13: Devoted Drivers
194 SS/David Alexander Liu **196** Volvo Press Room **197** Volvo Press Room **198** AP/Remy de la Mauviniere **199** Wikimedia **200** Wikimedia/IFCAR **201** © Mercedes-Benz USA 2007 **202** SS/Natalia Bratslavsky **203** AP/File, Adam Rountree

At the Smithsonian
208bl Division of Work and Industry, NMAH/SI [#2003-19242] **208tr** Division of Work and Industry, NMAH/SI [#2007-8611] **209** Division of Work and Industry, NMAH/SI [#45576-A] **210** Division of Work and Industry, NMAH/SI [#2005-5764] **211t** National Air and Space Museum/SI [#79-832] **211b** Smithsonian Photographic Services [82-8967]

Cover Art
Front © Automobili Lamborghini Holding S.p.A
Back Division of Work and Industry, NMAH/SI [#88-6486]

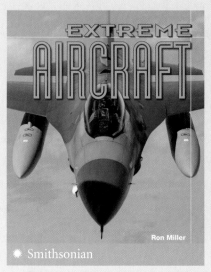
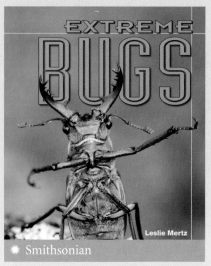
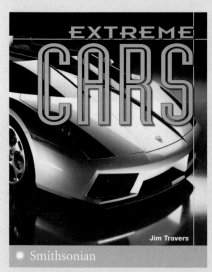
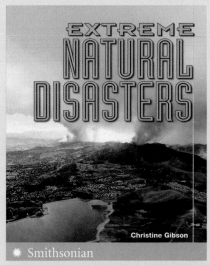